WHY IS GRANDMA NAKED?

CARING FOR YOUR

AGING PARENT

ELLEN POBER RITTBERG

Library of Congress Control Number: 2021901001

ISBN 978-0-578-82862-6 (paperback)
ISBN 978-0-578-84729-0 (ebook)

This is a book of humor. The information contained in this book is for discussion only. Nothing contained herein intends to be or is purported to be legal, medical, educational, psychological or any other form of advice. Before taking any action related to a person's mental or physical health or welfare, you should seek the help of professionals as you deem necessary.

This book is dedicated to the memory of my mother, a great, dignified lady who I was blessed to live with for her final six years. If she was still alive, I'm fairly certain she'd be mortified that I'm sharing these strange-but-true examples from her life but after the initial shock, I know she'd approve. She was always proud of my accomplishments and supportive of my writing. And if I feel a pang of guilt, I'll tell my adult children to feel free to write a weird-but-true humorous self-help book about me. Lord knows, they already have *plenty* of material and I don't even think I've begun to decline. But then, again, I wouldn't necessarily know, would I?

TABLE OF CONTENTS

INTRODUCTION

"Not now." "What difference does it make?" "Leave me alone!" Sound familiar? It should. It's Elderspeak. Part trash talk, part teenage lingo, part Esperanto, it's the opposite of whatever you want your elderly parent to do. For example: Mom is overdue for a bathroom visit and you urgently (pun intended) need her to *go*. Or you've told Dad that his nasal canal is not the New York Finger Lakes, and you get . . . nothing, nada, or one of the above phrases.

This book is for anyone close, kind and responsible enough to step in to do the large, commendable thing that is the subject of this book: caring for a declining loved one. And please note: when I use the word "parent," I mean your mother, father, spouse, sibling, grandparent, great-grandparent, aunt, uncle, cousin, close friend, neighbor or any other human significant other. My street cred, if you will, is that I moved in to care for my mother when she began to decline and I remained there "in the trenches" so to speak for six years. For those who like reading author's backstories, I refer the reader to the back of this book. To save you the trouble: it details how, among other things, I became a better person while at the same time becoming a socially stalled adult.

In this book, I share what worked for me. I attempt to activate your funny bone when you've forgotten you had one. I also suggest what skills you need to master such as *learning not to cringe*. If you're starting late in the game, no worries. Hop on board. It's never too late to do the right thing.

As to the organization of this book: to paraphrase Oscar Hammerstein (I happen to be a Broadway junkie), let's start with the letter A! And please don't call me out if you see the same letter more than once. No, those chapters aren't about vitamins. I figure, if New York City has a 6½ Street, I can have a C2 or D3. But there's no chapter that starts with the letter Z. I couldn't think of any z words except zzzzz, which describes elderly parents' talent at falling asleep at the drop of a hat unless, of course, it's nighttime.

Please note: I do not profess to be an expert. I hold no degrees in gerontology, psychology or any other "ology." I share what I came to know as a daughter, layperson and caregiver/planner/chief decision maker. Going into this gig, I did have one small advantage: I'd had extensive contact with many senior citizens and the professionals who cared for them as part of my job. But that didn't help at all when I was dealing with my own parent.

Watching a parent age, decline, and fade daily and up close is humbling and sometimes even depressing. Looking back, I realized those many funny, memorable moments were worth sharing. Having my mother remain at home for the final phase of her life was well worth it for both of us. I also know I couldn't have done it without putting the necessary supports in place.

Each parent's course of aging is different, but there are many common threads. I have attempted to draw them together here. And please note: This book offers no advice—legal or otherwise. My use of the imperative voice, "do and be," are used for comedic effect. I share what worked for me and what didn't. This is the book I wish I had while going through those often-fraught years.

Shall we begin? Yes, let's!

I suggest viewing your life as a road. You are the driver and the navigator. (Or is it that your parent is the car and you are the road? Whatever. Alas, I never took an advanced metaphor course!) At first, the road will have no signs and will be as dark as the plague in the

Moses story. So, baseline, going in you should know *it's hard caring for an elderly parent.* To succeed, you need to have rock-solid commitment and flexibility. *But the good news is, the job doesn't require a high IQ or any advanced skills. It requires heart.*

And a cautionary note: if you think your life will be a wild, wacky improvised jaunt like those road-trip-with-declining-dad movies, I say no. BIG NO. If you haven't seen such a movie, please don't.

This book is the same genre as my previous humorous self-help book, *35 Things Your Teen Won't Tell You, So I Will* (Turner Publishing). I'd be lying if I said that being interviewed on television and digital and print media and *Reader's Digest* asking me to write a piece wasn't thrilling. (Alas, my fragile ego compels me once a year to google my name.) Okay, fine, yes, so maybe it's more than once a year.

Skip around if you wish. And please, laugh at the funny parts: preferably out loud and in a public place—it's a good advertisement. And lastly, I offer you a hearty, heartfelt cheer: You, *yes, you can do this.* Your efforts, even the well-intentioned failures, are commendable and worthy of admiration.

Please note: Regarding pronouns, sometimes I use he, she, her, him, they or them and it may not necessarily mean I am speaking about just one parent. Never having been a grammar nerd, I never much bought into the term "pronoun-verb agreement."

ABOUT OUR PARENTS' GENERATION: SOME GENERAL POINTERS

1. Some of our parents had what used to be called "deprived childhoods." If you are unsure what that means, think of a Charles Dickens chimney sweep but eliminate the chimney.

Then, gaze out to some far-off place when your mom slides the entire contents of a restaurant wicker basket of Melba Toast into her purse.

2. Even if your parents were as emotionally closed off as Fort Knox, when they decline, all their issues, all their *stuff*, comes out…and the form it takes is *weirdness*.

3. "Put it back on the shelf, Dad. It's not free," is a new rote phrase I suggest you memorize. Un-empathetic types may regard taking other's belongings as flagrant theft. Which is why having an attorney's phone number handy whenever your parent is near merchandise that is not locked up, nailed down or adequately secured makes sense. But, hey, look, the good news is: it's not like Mom or Dad have suddenly embraced Communism.

4. If your parents could have taught a master class, "Parenting Without Visible Displays of Affection," and you now think they will suddenly turn all kinds of warm and fuzzy, to use a popular Brooklynism: fuhgeddaboutit. My family members' repeated attempts to kiss or hug Mom were met with "Don't kiss me. I have a cold." This led to a standard warning given to all future family members: *"Don't touch Mom/Grandma!"* I'm convinced Mom would have won the *Guinness Book of World Records* for Person Whose Cold Lasted the Longest if there was such a category. (Hey, they have a category for the Person Whose Hiccups Lasted the Longest. So why not?)

5. If, prior to their decline, your parent liked to play musical tables and chairs in restaurants (asking to change tables after your party was seated), there's good news: now your parent will be fine wherever the host or hostess puts you. But now it's you who's requesting the change because you're worried Mom or Dad will catch a draft.

AND A BRIEF DESCRIPTION OF MY MOM BEFORE HER DECLINE

Since I use Mom for almost every example I give, herein is the *CliffsNotes* version of Mom:

A motherless child, Mom learned early on not to make waves. She rarely gave unsolicited opinions, and she was extremely secretive. If I told her about a conversation I had and she felt the other person learned more about me than I learned about them, I was a chump and a blabbermouth. Mom may have been a housewife, but I'm convinced she missed her calling as a CIA or MI-5 operative. You know that line in *Casablanca* (or some other old movie) where Peter Lorre says, "I know nothing!" (actually, he said, "I know naaaaah-thing")? That was Mom's family credo, or, "Loose lips sink ships."

Because of Mom's early difficult life, she was stoic and hard to read. Once I accidentally closed the car door on her hand, and *she did not even flinch*. Although she wasn't a betting woman, she'd mastered an essential gambler's trick: the poker face. Mom was forever telling me to "Smile only with your mouth, like Greta Garbo." To which I responded, "Mom, Greta Garbo became a recluse when she aged." Not surprisingly, Mom looked decades younger than her age. And I don't.

Mom had trouble smiling naturally, even when posing for family photographs. Before one of my children's weddings, I had to beg her to smile naturally (or more accurately, I coerced her, saying, "Mom, you're going to ruin the pictures if you smile like Joker!"). The strange thing is, Mom wasn't an unhappy person. In her early eighties, Mom lost a considerable amount of weight, "after the doctor gave me a scare," and she became a fashion plate of sorts, wearing tastefully embellished sweaters and denim outfits even into her nineties. Strangers would stop us on the street and in restaurants to say how beautiful Mom was.

A world traveler who loved exploring new cultures, Mom enjoyed cruising to far-off places such as Ushuaia. (And FYI: Ushuaia is the southernmost city in the world. Yeah. *I hadn't heard of it either.*) At age eighty-nine, Mom rafted down the Snake River despite not knowing how to swim. (True, there were only baby currents in that part of the river. But still!)

A voracious reader, Mom enjoyed sharing what she knew, but only if she was asked to. And there's one thing I *still* can't figure out: although she didn't subscribe to newspapers, didn't use a computer or own an android or iphone, she was always the first person to tell me about breaking news!

TO KNOW: STRESS AND ANXIETY COME WITH THE TERRITORY

Rich or poor, city dweller, suburban dweller, exurban dweller, cave dweller: dealing with your aging diminished parent is stressful and sometimes, flat-out scary. And unless you are a Zen master or a totally chill, Type B personality, there will be moments that approximate the hapless victims in Alfred Hitchcock movies. (For those in need of a visual aid, I refer you to the movie poster for the movie *Vertigo* where the figure is upside down and spinning.) The good news is, your stress level *will* diminish (until the next crisis, that is).

So, sit back or walk, stream something funny, visit a dog park even if you don't have a dog, get a massage, or do whatever helps you to de-stress. And smile because caring for your parent will make you a better person even if you thought you were already a good person. And consider this: for centuries, adult children across our planet have cared for their elderly parents (*except in those cultures where they believed leaving Mom or Pop on a mountainside to be consumed by wolves or other local beasts was a viable plan*).

AND A BRIEF WORD ABOUT
A POSITIVE TREND

There is a social movement called Aging in Place, the aim of which is to keep elderly parents in their homes. This makes perfect sense. Most of our parents don't want to leave what is known and familiar. The good news is, some municipalities have programs to encourage that. However, to successfully age in place, there must be a solid support system and serious financial numbers-crunching. And for many people, it still isn't feasible.

A REALITY CHECK MAY BE IN
ORDER. I KNOW I NEEDED ONE

I'm a Baby Boomer. Because some of us erroneously believe we ducked the aging bullet, we can be ridiculously unrealistic about what we are capable of doing, energy-wise. But then we get a reality check. Parts of our bodies wear out or break down. *(Thank you, bionic hip!)* and we discover it takes longer than expected to heal and get back to snuff *(whatever snuff is)*. None of us have the same energy we had in our twenties, even if our grown children describe us as Energizer Bunnies.

In my case, when Mom began to decline, I did every single thing that needed doing alone and I continued to, for a long period of time. Foolishly.

Chapter 1

A: BE THE ALPHA DOG

Whether you live with your aging parent or not, you need to be in the driver's seat (even if you don't drive). From Day One, develop an appropriately authoritative, booming voice. Think James Earl Jones. Think a five-star general (same thing). Be that Alpha Dog. If you choose to do this (strains of *Mission Impossible* should play here), you'll have the unenviable job of telling Mom what she can and can't do. There is one caveat, though: if her judgment is still largely intact, she may challenge your Alpha Dog status and fight to have someone more Gummy Bear-like replace you. And if there is no Alpha Dog, chaos will set in. Guaranteed.

Chances are, in the beginning of her decline, she'll tell you what to do, and you may actually do it—even though it makes no sense. After all, she is your parent. Respect may at first motivate acceding to your parent's wishes, however ridiculous. But you must come to your senses. Developing dictatorial tendencies is a must. Once you bark out enough commands, it will become second nature, and you'll have little or no angst, *agita*, or guilt over the New You. In short: Become a Parent Whisperer without the whisper.

TO KNOW: THE BLOWBACK WILL COME

If you tell Mom what she can and cannot do, she will give you a what-for, even if she didn't previously major in Sarcasm 101. If your parent is very unhappy with your dictates, she may insult you and point out your character deficiencies (all of which you are aware of and may still be working on). If your parents weren't The Compatible Couple of the Century, she will tell you that you are just like the other parent.

It is strongly recommended that you don't debate the issue. Even if the insults hit the mark (ouch!), consider it water off a duck's back and paddle on. No one wants someone else to be master of his or her ship/car/shower, least of all one's adult child, with whom there is *A History.*

TO KNOW: YOUR PARENTS ARE LIKE TODDLERS

Your parents are just like toddlers. How so, you may ask?

a. They become increasingly more and more blithe and indifferent about their safety, proper conduct, regular hygiene and the rules of etiquette.

b. They do not like having boundaries set because they think they are in charge. Allowing them to hold fast to certain false beliefs and fantasies to the greatest extent without putting them in harm's way is highly recommended.

c. They will raise their voices and scream. The only difference being, unlike toddlers, they will not temporarily turn blue unless they have breathing issues.

AN EXAMPLE

You tell your parent to go to the bathroom. He adamantly refuses. If you insist, he will get annoyed. If you don't insist, to use the vulgar vernacular: s—happens. So, insist, order and demand. And prepare to deal with the flak. If you are sufficiently stern and insistent, he may comply with your request in a time-bound way. And time *is* of the essence.

Ironically, Mom's favorite quotation was, "Always visit the bathroom when arriving at a destination and when leaving." She learned that from reading Katharine Hepburn's autobiography—Katharine's father was a urologist. (Mom loved reciting her favorite movie stars' pearls of wisdom.) To this day, I'm not sure if Mom's (mostly) near-miss bathroom experiences were because of her declining memory or because she'd always been late to everything! But know: digging in your heels will help you maintain successful Alpha Dog status.

TO REITERATE: USE THE IMPERATIVE FORM OF ADDRESS

Insisting and commanding are not the same as cajoling, which works as well as wearing unlined kid gloves in subzero weather. When you need your parent to do something, your sentences should be short and clipped and your voice quality should most closely resemble a puppy trainer's. Use one of the following words: *go, do or don't*. Folding your arms and cultivating a sufficiently grim demeanor helps too. But don't use phrases like *pretty please with sugar on top*. If you do, it will lower the likelihood of being complied with.

Chapter 2

B1: BE SENSITIVE ABOUT YOUR PARENT'S THINGS

Because aging parents' lives change in unanticipated, often extreme ways, they are not always Mr. or Ms. Congeniality. As they see it, people who have no business tampering with them or their property do, with impunity. And, understandably, adjusting to this new state is hard, especially if their cognition is largely intact. Arguments will ensue about things we might consider unimportant but to our parents are a *Big Deal*.

AN EXAMPLE: THE ADJUSTABLE DRIVER'S SEAT MINI-DRAMA

When Mom was still driving, I drove her car because my SUV was too high for her to step safely into. Also, my car looked *way* better than hers. (Her car had so many dents and dings, it resembled a Picasso sculpture.) I adjusted her driver's seat. I couldn't help myself. Although Mom had the erect posture of someone decades younger and had at one time been the same size as me, she had shrunken considerably, and I now towered over her. *(And FYI: this Shrinking Parent phenomenon is almost never perceived by adult children who see their parents often.)*

Changing the position of Mom's driver's seat set her off, despite my assurances that I would move it back to its original position. I confess. I often forgot to change it back. Who said middle-aged children don't have our own memory issues? Okay, fine. I always forgot, and Mom would call me out and tell me I was careless. I owned up and apologized. But this did not placate her because I had triggered her elephant-in-the-room-sized anxiety. *Or was I engaging in that passive-aggressive rebellious teenage redux dance all adult children do when they return to their childhood homes? Do I have to answer that?*

I don't know what Mom thought would happen if she tried to change the driver's seat back to its original position. Squirrels popping up from below the seat? Looking back, those dust-ups could have been avoided if I had forced myself to remember how important it was for Mom to feel she controlled her environment. Our parents will do everything in their diminishing power to try to gain control over their ever-changing lives. It makes sense.

Chapter 3

B2: BOUNDARIES: HUH? YOUR AGING PARENT HAS NONE

I'll cut right to the chase here: very cognitively declining aging parents have no boundaries. Repeat. *None.* Their club is large and non-exclusive. It includes parents who:

a. Were somewhat well-mannered but who, every now and again when no one was looking, spat onto the sidewalk (and here I share the Yiddish verb because its sound describes it so perfectly: *harruching);*

b. Were previously highly refined types who always placed a napkin in their laps and never had an etiquette lapse;

c. May have never read *Tiffany's Table Manners for Teenagers* but at least knew there was such a book and tried to act civilized; or

d. Were entirely boorish and never bought into the etiquette thing.

And, one day, you realize that your parent has moved from the a,b and c groups into the d group.

But not to worry. Their behavior isn't willful. Once you get over the initial shock, you will be surprised at how tolerant the world is.

If you are a card-carrying curmudgeon, you may even have to revise your negative view of humankind.

And if you still are finding it hard adjusting to your parent's new state, look of it this way: maybe she is going through a very-late-in-life crisis and is trying out a new image: a hippie-dippy, cast-care-to-the-wind type.

TO KNOW: THE ISSUE OF WIND

And speaking of wind, be aware: your parents will cut wind, but unlike most people, they will not beat a hasty retreat into another room or stare at the ceiling while in an elevator pretending it wasn't them who cut the cheesecake. No. Shame and propriety are now alien concepts to them.

AN EXAMPLE

Years ago, my father, who had been quite civilized before his decline, became etiquette-challenged. One evening, while standing in the aisle of a crowded commuter train, Dad (how shall I put it delicately?) *let one rip*. The man whose face was closest to the offending source (my father's posterior, Dad was very short) irately tapped him on the shoulder and threatened to punch his lights out. To quote my mother at the time: "Your father is not a well man!" Oddly—or not so oddly—when my father told me the story, he laughed heartily and was not the least bit embarrassed!

Chapter 4

B3: PARENTS' BODIES AND THEIR BODILY FUNCTIONS

Your parents may not understand how their behavior affects themselves and others, but you need to. And preferably soon after that first cringe-worthy moment occurs.

DO I HAVE TO SAY THIS WAS MY MOTHER?

Remember as a child, if you lived near a beach in the Western hemisphere you were told that if you dug deep enough, you'd reach China? And do you also remember resolutely digging deeper and deeper with an impressive level of concentration? Well, the depths and heights some parents reach into their bodily recesses to get to the buried treasure is roughly equivalent to a child's sand-digging.

Be prepared. Your parents' fascination with their body's orifices will lead them to explore them to the point of making themselves bleed. Their noses, gums and teeth are great favorites. To put a funny spin on it: perhaps they are engaging in what used to be a popular medical practice: bloodletting (which, just to trot out a useless piece of information, was widely practiced during Shakespeare's time). And if you've considered strategically placing a toothpick or toothbrush within their easy reach to lessen their need to dig in, *give it up, please! Spare yourself the wasted effort and toothpicks. They won't use it.*

TO KNOW

To your parent, the human nostril is not something to be wiped periodically. It is now a top *Travel and Leisure* destination. If you've previously been unsure which human body part is connected to what other body part, wonder no more! Instead, spend a few moments observing Dad practicing The Scientific Method. (Remember middle school science class where you learned to formulate a hypothesis, test it out and then come to a conclusion?) Your parent's conclusion is they like having their fingers up there!

Putting an absurd spin on this: maybe they just want to give their fingers a workout. Consider their behavior a variant form of chair yoga, and unless they are sitting in the middle of an airport or a posh restaurant, ignore them and let them go about their business. And definitely don't think about berating them. Others will catch on and (it is hoped) respectfully look away. Or, if you are in public, put some obstruction in others' line of sight so as to not spoil their dining pleasure. Hunch over and stare intently at your plate. And don't look up, unless your parent is predisposed to choking.

In short, the first time you see your parent or loved one doing something truly gross, simply tell yourself to get used to it. And understand: their conduct is not a willful gesture. It is a return to our essential and basic evolutionary animal selves. Think of your parent as a modern-day John Rambo in *First Blood*. He is merely thinking up makeshift ways to cause pain to himself and extreme discomfort to others using what is the most primitive but effective tool known to man: a finger.

Chapter 5

C1: CALL UPON OTHERS

Through time, you will discover that not all of your parent's needs can be met by you, even if you decide to move in and pitch a pup tent beside his bed.

AN EXAMPLE:

Your parent gets a bad eye infection. The eye drops have to be dispensed multiple times a day for several days. The eye infection gave you no advance warning: health stuff rarely does. The aide, if your parent has one, is not permitted to do it. And you can't be there all the time to do it. So, what do you do? Be smart. Ask someone suitable. And along with this request, make certain to emphasize *how much Dad needs that person and how important the task is.* Or even if a task isn't that large and important, make it sound as if it is.

Assuming the person says yes and it works out all right, congratulate yourself. You've acknowledged that you're not the only person who does things for your parent. This is a Big Deal. This is progress. Your parent reaps the benefit of having more than just you in this budding support system. Soon after your successful initial ask, acknowledge how wonderful it was they did this large, important thing, and if need be, lay it on thick. And if emoting profusely is not something you are adept at, I suggest taking acting lessons.

Equally important: enlist that same person again without too much time elapsing between Ask One and Ask Two. If you are lucky, that family member will continue to pitch in without being asked. Think of them as a change of scenery (you being the regular scenery, that is). No offense but, like all-news radio, you're probably not all that interesting to be with all day, all the time!

There is a practical reason for enlisting others sooner rather than later. If you never asked them to do hands-on things, they may refuse you when you finally do because they don't feel comfortable. And they'll also refuse you for non-hands-on things because for too long you've put out a message that they aren't needed.

TO KNOW: PEOPLE DON'T READ MINDS

Don't expect others to read your mind unless they are famous mind readers. They don't know you've reached your near-breaking point and are hanging on by a hair.

TO ALSO KNOW:

Expect those people you call upon that first time to act annoyed and put-upon—especially if they feel you did not give them enough advance notice. They are working off an erroneous belief that you control the timing and frequency of your parent's health crises. Disabusing them of that notion is a must!

TO KNOW: A HALO ISN'T ATTRACTIVE. NO OFFENSE.

Painting a halo around your head is not recommended. Besides, halos don't look attractive on anyone (except saints and gods in religious paintings). Moreover, by doing everything yourself, you deny others that warm and fuzzy feeling that comes from doing the right thing for a loved one.

If there are no other siblings or close family members who can help, but your parent is fortunate enough to have caring neighbors who wish to help, by all means, let them (and possibly, if you have the resources, offer to pay them if they are expending time, energy and/or gasoline—but only if they won't feel offended by your offer). But you should know: almost always, one family member does the lion's share of caregiving. Which leads to:

Chapter 6

C2: CALL ON OTHERS: THEY'RE NOT CHOPPED LIVER

As good a job as you think you're doing for your parent, someone is better at some of those tasks than you. It's far, far, better to get off your too-high martyr's horse—if that's what you're on—and besides, saddle sores hurt. See what it's like at ground level. No offense, but you're not good at everything! No one is.

TO KNOW: EVERYONE HAS SOMETHING TO BRING TO THE TABLE

Unless you have an identical twin (and, even then, no twins are exactly alike), each adult child has something different and valuable to bring to the table: themselves. One child may be good at computer things. He or she can bring an iPad or laptop to show your parent enlarged photographs, videos, cool Instagrams, TikToks or what-have-you. One sibling may be able to do arts and crafts projects. Another sibling may be handy at putting things to-gether or making minor modifications to the home. Still another family member may be taller than you and, thus, more suited to being the Main Lightbulb Changer. There's no better way to put one's skills to use and feel good about oneself than attending to one's aging parent—even if some adult children don't see it that way at first.

And don't forget the one-off tasks. If you hate hiring a plumber to do something minor, enlist the sibling who knows how to unbend a wire hanger to extract a glob of hair that looks like something wild, slimy and alive from a clogged drain (i.e., hair slime). Of course, if you have water streaming from your toilet out your front door—this really happened to me once but not in connection with an elderly parent—expert help is needed.

Unless you like feeling like Jim Carrey precariously balancing too many plates on a tray, give yourself a break (and a hand) and enlist others. And if you're not sure what skills others have, find out. Who said adult siblings or even spouses know everything about each other?

TO KNOW: DON'T BE EAGER TO EXCLUDE OTHERS IN YOUR CLUB

When I was in the fifth grade, comedian Allan Sherman wrote a song about Rat Finks, a toy composed of what I think was a real raccoon tail. (Don't hate us, please, animal rights activists. We were very young and un-woke!) The rule was, if you bought a Rat Fink and played handball with us at recess, you could be in our club. (Clearly, our club wasn't that exclusive.)

By the same token, becoming a member in the non-exclusive club of Mom's and Dad's Helpers should be encouraged. There shouldn't be foolish, rigid rules of exclusion. Of course, there are exceptions. Adult children who were abused or neglected can also be excluded if they wish to be excluded. I've met adult children who, even though their parent was very deficient, wanted to do something and did. I marvel at that. But if they don't want to participate, I understand that, and I certainly do not judge them.

TO REITERATE: IT'S LONELY BEING A LONE WOLF

Don't—and I repeat—do not fall into doing everything yourself. Others don't even have to be good or better than you at something. Passable is good enough. And ask them even if they grouse, act cantankerous and suggest exploring nursing homes (even though your aging parent isn't nursing home material). And don't be surprised when those non-participating adult children come around. Or, if they don't, at least you can say you tried.

TO KNOW: IF YOU ARE AT THE BREAKING POINT, TELL YOUR FAMILY

You must explicitly ask others for help. Verbalize *your* needs. Chances are, if you are the main caregiver, you stepped into the breach when you saw you were needed, and remained there. And to be sure, there are days you do feel overwhelmed. But chances are, you forge on. But realize that sometimes you need help!

Chapter 7

C3: PURGE THE WORD CONVENIENT FROM YOUR VOCABULARY

Nothing about your aging parent is convenient. Much of it is not fun and games, either. Mom's or Dad's needs will disrupt social schedules—guaranteed. If you can't see it through to do the hands-on things, lend an empathetic ear to the caregiver. And if you don't live anywhere near, be a problem solver. Deal with an erroneous bill that requires time and causes aggravation. And if you can't do tasks using a phone or computer, pay someone who can. At least you will have taken one thing off the most-involved caregiver's plate.

TO KNOW: CHOOSE SOMETHING THEY'LL FEEL GOOD ABOUT DOING

If you don't want to be chronically angry, ask the sibling or other significant person to do something they'll likely agree to do. And here, personalities come into play. While most adult children will rise to the occasion when a major crisis happens, some may draw a line about what they will and won't do and how often they'll do it. By the same token, your requests for assistance should not just be for one-off, unimportant tasks. If you make other family members feel superfluous and unimportant, you can bet dollars to donuts they'll do little or nothing.

To underscore: You can't do it alone. Cannot. Should not. Would not. And, yes, I am a huge fan of Dr. Seuss.

Chapter 8

D1: DON'T IGNORE THE DOWNWARD DECLINE

It's not uncommon for adult children to be in denial that Mom or Dad is not doing well. It's painful to watch our parents be less than they once were. And often it's hard to recognize the decline. Many times, the decline is subtle, especially in the beginning (unless they've had a medical episode, such as a stroke or other serious illness). But if you are too busy to notice, it *will* come back to bite you. By then, their needs will be large and Technicolor bold. And (to quote Edgar Allan Poe), their issues will come rap, rap, rapping at your door. (Or is it tap, tap, tapping? Whatever.)

Here's another job to add to your task wheel: observe your parent. Analyze what you think those changes mean. Seek outside professional help if you don't have a definitive answer. Don't ignore what you see, hear or are told by reliable third-person sources. *Elderly parents are like hothouse plants. Give them the right care, and they may not necessarily thrive, but you will have given them the best life they can have, given the dimensions of their decline.* Ignore such signs and parents will decline even faster than they might otherwise have.

Chapter 9

D2: THE LITTLE THINGS ARE BIG THINGS

The little things and the big things you do matter mightily to your declining parent. Sometimes equally.

AN EXAMPLE

Mom liked blueberries. She ate them every day without fail. This might have been because Mom always wrote down things the television doctors said were good for her. (She did live to age 95, so maybe I should be eating blueberries daily and watching doctor shows?) Or perhaps she just liked the taste of blueberries. Consequently, there always had to be blueberries in the house. Since I was the Shopper-In-Chief (read that: the only shopper), it was up to me to make certain Mom always had her blueberries. Which I faithfully did, ninety-nine percent of the time. But that one time I forgot to replenish Mom's blueberries, the first question Mom asked when I returned home was, "Where are the blueberries?" This was proof Mom had begun to decline. If she hadn't, she would have asked me how my day was, and *then* she would have berated me for forgetting her blueberries.

When I said I'd forgotten her blueberries, she was furious. I felt terrible because, on that particular day, I was too tired after my long commute to do grocery shopping. And it was too late to get anything delivered. The takeaway is: don't forget the blueberries.

TO KNOW:

When elderly folks decline in all kinds of ways, mealtimes become the high points of their day if their appetites are intact. And if meals always were the high point of their day, meals will become an even-higher point!

TO KNOW: ROUTINES LOWER YOUR PARENT'S STRESS AND, THUS, YOURS

Another takeaway: at first, I didn't understand quite how important Mom's routines were. Older, frail, declining adults rely heavily on their unvarying routines and favorite foods. So, to the greatest extent possible, try not to get in the way of them. Come to think of it, maybe that isn't so weird. I, for one, feel out of sorts without my morning scooped-out whole wheat bagel and two hard-boiled egg whites! And I've been like that for the past thirty plus years.

Chapter 10

D3: GIVE YOUR PARENTS THEIR DUE (THEIR FREAK FACTOR)

We never know how much time we have left on this planet. (Well, most of us don't. Crystal-ball readers, anyone?) At this stage of their lives, our folks are entitled to be whoever they've become. To be alive at their advanced age means they did *something* right, even if it is not always apparent to us what that some*thing* is.

So, here's my pitch: unless they create extreme bodily havoc to themselves or others, let their freak flags fly proud and high.

TO KNOW: ACCEPT THE STRANGENESS. IT'S NOT GOING AWAY

If, for your sanity, you're able to find your declining parent's eccentricities amusing, that's a huge plus. And if their conduct doesn't harm them or place them in the criminal justice system, let them (to quote Nike) Do It. Double points if you can adopt the proper spirit and celebrate their eccentricities. Acknowledge that some of what they do has a deep-seated origin. You may not understand what that origin is unless you are a trained therapist. And even then, you might not! Some parents who suffer from dementia love ripping paper. Don't ask me why. Maybe they're subconsciously preparing to move from the world of the continent to the incontinent, and are just paper-training themselves? Oh well, that's the best explanation I could come up with!

Four common things declining parents do that their children find perplexing:

1. Letting their natural odors and effusions rip or come out.
2. Stripping down to their birthday suits.
3. Conning their children into believing their alternate reality.
4. Creating fictional scenarios about people they have little or no relationship to.

Chapter 11

D4: DESIGNATED HITTER

There's a term they use in the American League: designated hitter—or I think they do. *(Me, I go to baseball games to get my once-a-year nitrite hot dog fix.)* That person is also called The Closer, i.e. the one person who can clinch the win. Here, I use that term to mean the person who gets the job done, and if you're reading this book, you're likely that person. And it doesn't rotate, either. You're "it" as they say in the game of Tag. No surprise there. Even before your parent's decline, you were the family member who did whatever was needed.

Why is it that whenever there is more than one adult child, one child does the lion's share? In my case, was it because I was the middle daughter and the peacemaker? Or was it because I'd been the weak, runty infant with dietary problems that required Mom to boil my milk three times? Maybe. Or, as Mom liked to say: *"Whatever."*

Generally speaking, the siblings who do less than the primary caregiver child appreciate that sibling. And the greater their understanding of the toll caregiving takes on the Designated Hitter, the greater the chance they will pitch in more. Which means sometimes they have to be educated about what it's like in the trenches.

Chapter 12

E1: ELEVATED STATUS COMES WITH THE TERRITORY

The aforementioned Designated Hitter is in an elevated position in the eyes of others. Other family members, including your adult children if you have any, and your siblings may tell you what a good child you are. However, you probably won't hear their hosannas. You're too busy caring for your parent.

The benefits of doing right by your parents are:

a. You are setting a great example for your children, who, when you show signs of decline, may rise to the occasion—*the occasion being you*;

b. However much your friends and some of your relatives respect you, they will respect you all the more because you haven't sought out their praise. And if you do seek out praise: *Really? Do you need to?*

You should feel good that you assumed the position of Chief Caregiver/Decision Maker because:

a. You believe in the concept of respecting your parents

b. Okay, so you don't totally buy into that concept, but you still love your parents

24

c. Once you embarked upon the journey, you decided there was no turning back

d. All or some of the above

e. You're not sure which of the above you agree with, but okay, one of the above

Chapter 13

E2: ENERGY OR THE LACK OF IT (EXCEPT AT NIGHT!)

As parents age, their nightly sleep routines change, often radically. For parents who have dementia, night becomes day and day becomes night; their sleep patterns most closely resemble those of owls and bats. One thing is for certain: whether they sleep at night or not, they will fall asleep during the day at the drop of a hat and it has nothing to do with your conversational skills. They'd fall asleep while meeting the Queen even if they were British. Why? Is it because they don't have the energy reserve that most physically active and mentally with-it younger folks do? Yes. (And here, I make a prediction: Napping rooms will be created for workers who are responsible for caring for their parents. And those rooms will be used to full capacity and then some.)

So, forgo buying expensive opera, theater, concert or ballet tickets. Or, if your parents insist on attending, try to find a seat with a partially obstructed view—a large pillar is best. This way, no one will notice that your parent missed those gorgeous Don Quixote ballet pas de deux. Or choose a seat far enough back so that the performers' eyes won't hinge upon them. *And obviously, if your parent snores, avoid public performances altogether.*

TO KNOW

Some cognitively declined parents scream at night (and day, for that matter). If yours don't, or rarely do, consider yourself fortunate. If they do, it would be wise to invest in a good pair of noise-cancelling headphones. Even better: pay someone to soundproof the walls.

Chapter 14

E3: EVERYTHING IN THEIR LIVES IS A BOOK. OPEN IT

As a child, did you ever hear the expression, "It's none of your B.I. business? It's for me to know and for you to find out." Well, unless your parents debriefed you on everything they own, you may have to reconstruct their past. Meaning, don't be so quick to throw things out. Ask questions if they're still able to communicate. Photographs (unless the volume is sky-high, and thus, a safety hazard) are theirs for the keeping—and yours and your siblings after they're gone. As to what constitutes a safety hazard, I suggest googling the words Collyer Brothers. (Okay, I'll tell you. Their clutter was so high that it killed them.) And maybe you don't want to throw out all those post-cards. It may jog and stimulate their memories. Or they'll give you some ideas for future travel destinations.

Some documents your parents need include:

1. Veteran's discharge papers
2. Naturalization papers
3. Wills and other legal documents
4. Driver's licenses
5. Social Security cards
6. Insurance policies

7. Third-party designee forms for insurance policies, etc.
8. Birth certificates
9. Death certificates of spouses
10. Cemetery plot information
11. Bank, stock and bond information
12. Deeds and mortgage documents
13. Objects that are of personal or material value to them or you, some of which you may not have even known about
14. Baptismal certificates or other religious documents

Finding these things may require going through every closet, drawer, purse, pocket or receptacle they have, even if they told you where *they thought* things are. Some of these documents may be of interest to you for no other reason than it was important to your parent. And sometimes, you and your parent may have some pleasant surprises.

AN EXAMPLE

Excavating a small closet sky-high with clutter in Mom's guest bedroom, I found some traveler's checks. Mom couldn't remember when she'd purchased them or what her travel destination had been but that didn't matter. They were still usable. Because Mom was still in a very early stage of her decline, she was able to spend the money however she wanted to. Found money!

TO KNOW: TAKE HEART! THE CLUTTER PROJECT CAN BE TACKLED

If your parent was a Depression-era (or other era) pack rat, there are companies that will comb through your parent's belongings.

Some are bonded, licensed and insured. If you choose to do it yourself, don't forget to look under every piece of furniture and beneath and behind each drawer! And remember: if you have questions about any personal, financial or health information and your parent can still provide details, ask them now. Memory loss is not reversible.

TO KNOW: YOU MAY UNEARTH THINGS. MYSTERY SOLVED!

While delving through the mountain of paper, you may discover:

a. Old love letters from people who may or may not be the person who subsequently became the person you *thought* was your parent

b. Old photographs of Mom or Dad with people you don't recognize and they look *way happier* than you ever saw them look

c. Pins, awards and certificates of accomplishments

d. Diplomas, or lack thereof

e. Old address books

f. Cancelled checks

g. Things they wrote down, such as what some television doctor said, which may be meaningful only because they are in your parent's handwriting

h. Old greeting cards from family members and others

i. Anything that reveals a family secret that you didn't know about

Asking them about any of the above may stir up some memories. It also might expand their conversational repertoire. (For all you know, they led a secret, exciting life. And a drumroll here: it could lead to a successful reality show, *Family Secrets Revealed*!)

Ah, memories, which, if your parents still remember, may contain a juicy fact or two—but there is a caveat. Some facts will only come out if:

1. They feel enough time has elapsed and
2. They feel it is safe to tell you or
3. You tease it out of them

An added bonus is that you get to hone your sleuthing skills. Shades of Nancy Drew!

Chapter 15

F1: FALLS

Falls are the most common cause of serious injury and death for elderly folks. Even if they survive a fall, they may never fully recover. Some falls can be prevented if caregivers are sufficiently vigilant. That vigilance includes making frail, elderly parents' homes safe. Specifically, you need to install grab bars in the bathroom and wherever else they are needed. Clear the floors of all obstructions. Small or low pieces of furniture, electrical wires, phone chargers…*anything* that can get in parents' paths when they walk should be removed.

Another reason our parents fall is, they are resistant to using canes and walkers. A social worker at an assisted living facility once told me the single most important reason elderly folks are living as long as they are is walkers.

AN EXAMPLE

Once, when my mother had just begun to decline, I drove her to the local CVS. She told me to wait in the car—I was exhausted after my long commute home. I noticed as she walked into the store that her gait looked a tad unsteady. To convince her to use her cane, I told her I'd seen a man and a woman watching her as she entered the store. They had a worried look on their faces. It was as if they were telegraphing to me that they hoped I didn't allow my mother to walk around alone without *some* walking aide. (I really did see that couple. And our eyes really did meet, so I didn't have to fabricate the story.) Mission accomplished. Mom agreed to use a cane.

At some point, many parents graduate to walkers when canes no longer afford them adequate support. Sadly, some of them refuse to accept that they need to use a walker, even though their ortho-pedists said they should and even though they've broken some of their bones repeatedly. If your parent is memory-compromised, that complicates matters further. They may agree to use the walker, but then they forget to use it.

If you discover something around the house that could make your parents trip and fall, you need to hide it, or, better yet, remove it. If you ask them permission to take the object elsewhere, expect arguments and refusals. If you succeed in removing the object, regard your action as a victory. You may have spared your parent at least one incident of broken bones, hospitalization, rehabilitation, infection or worse. I once spirited a small but dangerous step stool out of Mom's house in a large trash bag—she was in another room and didn't see me taking it out. Trash bags come in very handy!

If your parent sees you taking something out in a large garbage bag, he will ask you what the bag contains. Tell him you are bringing food scraps to the compost heap. If he says that's impossible, the municipality doesn't have a composting site, tell him you've become very green and that you are headed to some other composting site. If he asks where, well… try to get the object out a different day.

If your parent does fall while with a caregiver, try to find out the sequence of events once the situation is stabilized. If Mom is able to tell you what happened, listen carefully. Dementia doesn't rob parents of their ability to tell the truth, as long as their short-term memory is still intact and they are verbally communicative.

One thing is almost certain: your parent is much more likely to fall when he is with a replacement caregiver. And there *will* be replacements. Reliable paid caregivers become ill or they have family members who do. When a temporary caregiver comes, you have to be *extremely clear* about what your expectations are, such as never leaving Mom in the bathroom alone. Tell them, "If the phone rings and you are taking care of Dad, let the phone ring. Don't answer it. Let it go to voicemail." (And the replacement caregivers may still ignore what you've told them.) Tell them what Mom eats and can't eat. Some elderly parents have swallowing and choking issues or allergies. Write detailed lists and walk them through the lists. Tell them they must keep a detailed log of all of the day's events, including the poop scoop.

The worst replacement caregiver Mom had was the one who called me on the phone to tell me Mom had fallen and that her leg was bleeding.

This was our verbatim conversation:

Replacement caregiver: Your Mom fell. Her leg is bleeding.
Me: Is it still bleeding?
Caregiver: Yes.
Me: Did you try to get it to stop bleeding?
Caregiver: No. (At this point, don't ask why not. This person is a screw-up, as you will learn as the conversation continues.)
Me: Is she sitting or lying down?
Caregiver: She's sitting.
Me: Press it to stop the bleeding.
Caregiver: Oh. Okay.
Me: Didn't you receive training in this?
Caregiver: Yes.

Me: And?

Caregiver: I don't remember what I'm supposed to do.

Later, when I asked the caregiver what happened, she told me that while bathing Mom, she decided to leave her alone in the bathroom, "to put the wet towel in your mother's bedroom," which makes no sense whatsoever! And I'd told her and written out very specific instructions that *under no circumstance* was she to leave Mom alone in the bathroom!

If a similar situation occurs, you will then race to your parent's home and take her to Urgent Care or an emergency room, whereupon she will get twelve stitches for what turns out to be a nasty laceration.

Another replacement aide flooded the kitchen within two hours of her arrival. That upset me far less than the caregiver who left Mom alone in the bathroom. Floors can be replaced. Parents can't.

Chapter 16

F2: FINDING A COMPANION: SING "MATCHMAKER"

There will come a time when your parent needs someone other than you in the picture. Whether that someone is part-time or full-time depends upon several factors:

1. How much you understand the decline
2. How much you are willing to accept the decline
3. Safety factors
4. Your parent's opinion on the subject
5. Financial resources
6. Your work schedule (if you work)
7. Your own needs

TO KNOW

If you underestimate the amount of time your aging parent needs assistance, it may be because you are too close to the situation to be objective. Or it could be because you're not thinking clearly, which is completely understandable—in my case, stress makes me stupid. And some of the changes your parent is experiencing may be too subtle for your untrained eye to detect. Choosing an aide or caregiver is anxiety-producing. It's even more stress-producing when the need is pressing.

The two most common times you will interview potential caregivers are:

1. Mom or Dad is in a rehabilitation center or hospital and is due to be released. This is an optimal time because the rehab stint has bought you some time to find someone. Moreover, a staff social worker can help you figure out:
   a. The hours of care your parent need
   b. The kind of care they need

   Usually, social workers will also have the names of aide-staffing agencies they are familiar with. If you know someone whose elderly parent recently passed away and had a wonderful caregiver who is available, call them. If they're suitable, hire them. Then buy yourself a lottery ticket. It may be your lucky day.

2. Your parent currently does not yet need a full-time caregiver but you know he needs a responsible person in the picture. Applaud yourself if you follow through on this. You are approaching your parent's decline in a timely, proactive way. If the person you hire wishes to be described to others in a particular way such as companion or friend, use that word.

   Some houses of worship have lists of local caregivers and companions. While they may not screen those folks at a level you feel comfortable with, you might be able to check out the references on your own. That is how I found Mom's first part-time companion. Once that person begins working, you will get some feedback from your parent—unless he is non-verbal—or you may learn things from your parent's body language. If you have good intuition, the caregiver interview process will be far less fraught than if you are a "meh" judge of character.

Having gone through the process more than once, I discovered there were any number of kindly, well-qualified available people to care for Mom. If your aging parent is still cognitively "with it," then she should have the final say. Or, at the very least, she should be included front and center in the decision-making process.

TO KNOW

If the professional at a hospital or rehab facility thinks your parent needs someone in the picture for x number of hours, and you think your parent needs less hours, you should listen to that professional. *(To put it bluntly: they're right and you're wrong.)* If your parent is recovering from some kind of physical injury or fall and is not cognitively compromised, the amount of time the caregiver is needed each day may diminish as your parent grows stronger. And it's possible that your parent will have improved so much that she no longer needs that person. But usually, through time, he'll require more help, not less.

AN EXAMPLE OF THE CHOOSING PROCESS

Above all, the right companion must be a good fit. And that fit depends on your parent's caregiving needs and personality. When Mom only needed a companion for a few hours a day to help prepare lunch and provide companionship, Mom and I arranged to meet and interview Janet (not her real name) at a local pizza parlor. Janet drove and had her own car. This was important because Mom lived where there was no mass transportation or other convenient, affordable transportation. I'm not really sure how old Janet was, but it was a definite plus that she was sort-of Mom's peer. *My theory is, when you get to a certain age, anyone within twenty-five years of your parent's age is a peer.*

Janet was peppy and talkative, which was the opposite of Mom, who was reserved and quiet. Janet enjoyed talking about her family, which included her adult son who lived with her and had recently become engaged. Mom enjoyed hearing about the wedding preparations and Janet's full social life, which included ballroom dancing and yoga classes. In short, she opened up Mom's increasingly socially constricted world. For the three or four hours every day that Janet was there, Mom was stimulated and her life was enhanced. And to my great surprise, even though Mom had always spent her days alone, she enjoyed Janet's presence.

In short, Janet was a godsend. I had some (needed!) peace of mind while she was at Mom's house. There was one glitch, however: Janet sometimes wouldn't show up or she'd show up late because of some home or appliance maintenance problem. I'm sure her excuses weren't bogus but they were annoying nonetheless because I had to deliver the bad news to Mom. My important takeaway was, some parents may be receptive to people and experiences they would have not otherwise have been receptive to before. (Or possibly not, but it's always worth trying to add stimulating activities and people into your parent's life.)

Chapter 17

F3: WHEN NEEDS CHANGE, NOTICE IT AND ACT

The second time Mom was hospitalized for a fall, her gait remained unsteady even after intensive physical therapy. I recognized she needed someone with her all the time when I wasn't there and Janet, her part-time companion, didn't want to work more than four hours a day. Mom also had declined a tad more cognitively. She needed someone who would show up on time every day, barring a very large weather event or other cataclysm. I arranged for several potential caregivers to come to the rehabilitation center. There, we met the candidates together.

One woman was in her late thirties. She seemed nice and friendly enough, but was not well-groomed. She looked as if she had just fallen out of bed. That, coupled with the fact that she had never worked as an aide, knocked her out of the box.

The second woman we interviewed chatted with Mom about this or that and told Mom how beautiful she was. When the interview ended, she patted Mom on the top of her head. That, for my dignified mother (and me), was a deal breaker. Clearly, no one had warned her beforehand, *"Don't touch Grandma!"*

I was able to rule out another potential caregiver on the basis of a phone conversation. She had an extremely loud and abrasive voice, and (at that time) Mom wasn't hard of hearing. *Or at least I didn't think she was hard of hearing.* Moreover, the son of the previous person she had worked for told me she could chew anyone's ear off with her nonstop chatter. Had we hired her, I'm certain she would've gotten on Mom's nerves in record time.

The fourth woman, and the one we ultimately chose, was dressed neatly and appropriately. This played into the mix because she would be helping Mom dress each morning and taking her to senior citizen programs, and I wanted Mom to look the way she had always looked: neat, tidy and reasonably fashionable. Maria (not her real name) had a warmth that Mom and I immediately felt was genuine.

Although English wasn't Maria's native language, her English was good enough. Mom understood her. That she'd been a social studies teacher in her native country was a bonus. Mom was a current affairs buff. After chatting with us for a good twenty minutes or so, she confidently stage-whispered to Mom: "I think we're going to be friends." Even if those words were a bit over the top, they proved to be correct. She became Mom's full-time companion. She took pride in her work and always accorded Mom respect. Mom never got hurt under her watch. And she always showed up on time. When staff members at the senior citizen center told me how impressed they were by her attentiveness to Mom's needs, it validated that Mom and I had made the right choice.

She had one other important asset: she was a very good cook. This was important, as Mom was a somewhat finicky eater (as many frail elderly people are). And Mom still had a reasonably normal appetite.

Chapter 18

G: IF TRANSPORTATION IS IFFY, GET WHEELS

If your parent lives in an area that is underserved by public transportation, a caregiver who drives is a big plus. Mom's caregivers didn't. On numerous occasions, she and her caregiver waited long periods of time for the frequently late, chronically unreliable county paratransit van. This triggered their anxiety and mine because I was the backup driver. I also worked full-time.

On one occasion, the paratransit van didn't come at all. This resulted in a frenzied call from Maria. After a number of fruitless calls that went to voicemail, I found out that the bus had broken down and a replacement bus was not coming at all. I then retrieved Mom and Maria. If you opt for a non-driver, figure out the approximate cost of Ubers, Lyfts and taxis on a weekly basis. Then ask yourself if the cost of buying you and Mom (and her caregiver) happiness, mobility, social opportunities and tranquility is do-able and worth it.

Chapter 19

H1: YOUR LIFE MAY BE ON HOLD

Unless you are a psychic or a soothsayer, when you assume responsibility for your parent, you won't know how long you'll be doing it for. And chances are, in the beginning, you won't realize how time-intensive and emotionally-intensive caregiving is. Which is why, even if you're not normally a gym rat, it's important to get some physical activity each day. Even if it's just walking up and back on your parent's block, it's something. And don't be surprised if some kindly person stops and asks, "Would you like a ride? Is everything all right?" which, yes, really did happen.

If you can't leave your parent alone for any length of time, try to do something active in the house. Lie on your back on the floor and peddle your feet in the air. (The more sweat-producing, the better.) Or jog in place while Dad watches *Wheel of Fortune* unless your continual thumping sets him off. According to some famous superstar, lifting light weights for as many reps as you can will keep you jacked. *And if you don't know what reps or jacked is, ask anyone younger than yourself.*

TO KNOW

If you decide to move in with your aging frail parents, or they move in with you, not only will you not be (if you ever were) a social butterfly; you may become a Socially Stalled Adult, which actually

43

has its advantages. In your little warren, you may produce some great work of literature, art, science or philosophy. Or not!

AN EXAMPLE

In the first few years that I moved in with my mother, because I also had a full-time job and had not yet hired anyone to pitch in, I had precious little free time. But I was determined to use what I had to my advantage. That first year, I wrote my first non-fiction book and found a publisher. During those first two years, my art was included in two group art shows. Knowing my mother's peace of mind depended on my being there made me eliminate all but the most essential activities, except perhaps nail-biting and eating.

Chapter 20

H2: HEAT

As your parents' bodies age, their ability to withstand extreme heat or cold diminishes. Thus, a lack of heat or too much heat is not only uncomfortable, it can make your parent ill, or worse. For some reason, oil burners and water heaters have a habit of breaking down in the middle of the night. Therefore, you must develop a very specific skill: shuffle-walking zombie-like to let the repairperson in after being roused from your REM sleep without breaking your neck.

When you call the heating company, be firm. Tell the dispatcher that not only can the broken oil burner not wait until morning, it can't wait *at all*. And even if Mom swore you to secrecy that you wouldn't divulge her age, you must tell them Mom's age and tack on a few years for good measure. This is the opposite of what your parent may have done her entire adult life. (Once, I had a devil of a time registering Mom at a hospital she'd been at before because she'd shaved a few years off her age. But I digress.)

AN EXAMPLE OF KNOWING PEOPLE'S NAMES AND BOILER PARTS

In Mom's twilight years, I made certain to know all the people by name who maintained her house, including the heating company dispatcher. Because she knew me as a polite person (unlike some of the rude, irate callers), she always arranged for someone to come in a relatively time-bound way—*or at least before frostbite set in.* I knew them all. Go ahead. Test me. Kathy, the dispatcher. Chris, the senior technician, and anyone else who came to the house. Whenever I needed an emergency late-night visit, I knew exactly who to ask for. My sensible, house-savvy older sister instructed me to "always ask for the senior technician." If no senior technician was available, I'd let a newer technician come to Mom's house. Invariably, the oil burner would break down again, usually minutes after the repair truck sped away from Mom's home.

Remembering people's names, some of whom may have been coming to your parents' house for years, is important. Expressing heartfelt appreciation for a job well done helps too. They'll take the time to explain detailed crucial information, such as how to lower the hot water temperature so Mom won't scald herself!

View any and all people who can positively or adversely affect your parent's life as part of a larger constellation of your parent's caregiving team. Once, Kathy the dispatcher instructed me how to press the light on the oil burner—and miracle of miracles—the light went on and stayed on. Unfortunately, this only worked one out of every five times, but when it did, I was ecstatic. I had one less night of aggravation, sleep-deprivation and next-day grouchiness.

Also get to know the service history of each appliance, oil burner or assorted object that can and will die or break down. If nothing else, it will make you feel more on top of things!

TO KNOW: ASK THE PERSON WHO IS HOME-SAVVY

If you are not the savviest about home repairs, call upon the sibling or friend who is, especially home repairs that require a serious cash outlay.

AN EXAMPLE

When Mom's central air-conditioning system broke and could not be repaired, I immediately called my older sister. She wisely suggested that I purchase individual units for the rooms Mom spent time in. This was far less costly than replacing the entire system. This made perfect sense because anyone who'd buy the house in the future would most likely tear it down. And they did!

Chapter 21

I-1: ILLNESSES COME TO ROOST (OR RE-ROOST)

Almost any illness that a frail elderly parent contracts is serious or life-threatening. And their recovery tends to be slower than for a younger person. Being in a hospital, dehydration, Urinary Tract Infections (UTI's), etc. All of these things can cause normally cognitively older adults to become disoriented. Once when Mom was in the hospital, she began talking about going home to an address she hadn't lived at for sixty years. The doctor told me, "Get your mother out of here. She has hospital-induced dementia. She'll be fine once she gets home." And she was.

Hospitals are not hospitable to frail elderly parents (or anyone for that matter). Antibiotic-resistant bacterial infections pose an ever-present risk, particularly for immunocompromised elderly people. If the illness is bacterial, antibiotics could interfere with your parent's already-established medication regimen. I especially liked that Mom's primary care doctor's philosophy was, "Let's keep Mom out of the hospital."

AN EXAMPLE OF AN ANCIENT ILLNESS RETURNING

Up until Mom hit her nineties, she was reasonably healthy. She'd cracked her pelvis, and her ambulation was a bit iffy, but she'd dodged any bullets, so to speak. (Once, when she was heavier, a see-ing eye dog knocked Mom down, but she didn't break anything. She was just very embarrassed that she'd fallen.) But everything changed as she neared her ninetieth year. She fell. She broke her pelvis. She contracted pneumonia. She broke her hip. Upon her return from the hospital, she began coughing. She'd contracted whooping cough. And most likely, she contracted it while in the hospital. (And FYI: Mom certainly wasn't an anti-vaxxer. I don't think she was ever of-fered the vaccine.) Whooping cough is highly contagious, so whip out that mask even when there isn't a pandemic. Whooping cough is particularly dangerous to very young children, so if you see or live with your parent, don't plan on visiting the grandchildren any time soon thereafter.

AN EXAMPLE OF WEIRD INJURIES AND WOUNDS

Once, Mom nicked her leg on the point of a cardboard Kleenex box while sitting in my sister' car. (And yes, you read that right: *a Kleenex box.*) Mom had always been a slow healer, and advanced age made her an even slower one. And elderly folks' skin is thinner than non-elderly skin. The wound refused to heal. I worried that Mom would develop cellulitis. Mom's doctor refused to give her an antibi-otic because it would interfere with her anti-blood clotting medica-tion. Mom didn't develop cellulitis. But whatever it was that she had on her leg sure didn't look pretty!

Chapter 22

I-2: IMPULSE CONTROL? DON'T BET THE FARM ON IT

It's a funny thing. While not-very-cognitively declined parents might be able to have what sounds like a normal conversation about politics, the newest breakthroughs in medical science or any number of other subjects, that doesn't mean they're not impaired. It's a shame there's no consumer product that miraculously unfurls a fluorescent banner announcing "Mom's declining." Some adult children will know it instinctively, but only if they are also very lucky and very observant. But even if you don't figure it out right away, there are two things that tell you (to paraphrase Bob Dylan) the times they are a-changing.

1. Their impulse control has become iffy. This is subtle at first. Like outdated food, the decline may pass the smell test but still not be good. And,
2. Their judgment is off (which sounds the same as 1) but isn't.

AN EXAMPLE

My mother broke her hip late one night after falling while carrying a 12-oz. bag of Hershey's Kisses around her kitchen. Where was the walker? It was at the opposite end of her kitchen. I'm not sure if she'd forgotten to use it because the only thing she could think about was eating those Hershey's Kisses. The old Mom (un-declined Mom) would have never bought such a large bag of candy, much less eaten it late at night. Having lost a good deal of weight in her early eighties, she was almost pathologically afraid of gaining weight.

If I were able to construct Mom's interior monologue during her hip-breaking incident it would have gone something like this: "I want Hershey's Kisses. I want to scarf those suckers down now. I am taking them into . . ." (I am unsure where she was going with them, as she fell in the hallway outside the kitchen). She could no longer cause and effect. Nor could she calculate how many calories a bag of Hershey's Kisses had.

TO KNOW: IMPULSE CONTROL AFFECTS MOOD

If you've ever heard a wailing baby demand food, you may be prepared for your parent's heightened, raging need to be fed the min-ute they get hungry. Erase from your mind that once she could have written the book on dignity, restraint and deferred gratification in. I've wondered, is it because many frail elderly folks don't have much of a fat reserve? I don't know, and I was too tired or lazy to google it. But personally, as a middle-aged thin person who is frequently famished, I'd do anything short of stringing a wire between two sky-scrapers if I saw something yummy at the far end when my hunger alarm goes off. What I do know is, my elderly parent was not fun to be around when she wanted what she wanted at the moment she wanted it.

ANOTHER EXAMPLE

Before Mom's cognitive decline, she'd describe her hunger calmly. She'd say, "I don't know why I'm so hungry," but she never got bent out of shape if her hunger wasn't sated right away. If she was thirsty, she'd say in a polite tone of voice, "Would you mind getting me a glass of water?" No longer. Social niceties went straight out the window. If she asked for a particular food and it wasn't given to her in record time, she'd say, "What's taking you so long to get the . . . (fill in the blanks)?"

TO KNOW: THEY ASK, YOU DO. NOW!

If your parent asks you to change a light bulb, you must drop whatever you are doing, or else Mom will attempt to change the light bulb herself (with calamitous result). Which is why you'll assume one other new role: Mister (or Missus) Fixit.

Chapter 23

I-3: INCONTINENCE
(OR THE LACK THEREOF)

Even adult children who think they have their daily living skills down pat know there are moments when their own relatively reliable continence might fail (think: sneezing hard or laughing uncontrollably with a full bladder. Or, er, is that just me?). But, hopefully, those rare unfortunate experiences give us some insight into our parents' human-plumbing problems.

A signal moment in our culture occurred around a generation ago when June Allyson made Depends a household name. There's an irony there. The word "depend" suggests a certainty. But it also suggests a level of equivocation and ambivalence as in *"it depends." Do I need to go? Or don't I need to go?*

The toileting act is a highly complex task. It requires speed, manual dexterity, eye-hand coordination, ambulation and memory. The memory part is the trickiest part. Which means that the more time a person allows himself to do his business before the situation becomes (um) emergent, the greater the chance he will succeed. And be aware: aging kidneys and bladders are not very forgiving organs!

I'll state the obvious because it is easy to forget: the partial or total loss of ability to control one's personal plumbing plays an enormous part in an elderly parent's life. It affects the sense of self, health and the ease with which your parent can go about their day. And yours.

If you're not sure whether your parent requires Depends, even just as a back-up, then let us have *That Talk*. Which may lead to you having a different talk with your parent. And for that, you must acquaint yourself with (to pun it) the ins and outs of the human waste elimination process. But the long and short of it is, when nature calls, its call must be listened to! It's as fierce as the running bulls of Pamplona, and for elderly seniors it's just as rapid.

TO KNOW

Incontinence, it could be argued, is a natural state. Babies let it out with ease or with a squeeze. And, at some point your parents will do that too. And they won't even know they are doing it.

Can we get real here? There may come a time when you think your parent's face is contorted in pain. But you have simply caught her in the middle of the act. She is no longer embarrassed, and you shouldn't be embarrassed for her, either. What you might want to do is give a heads-up to other family members who don't realize Mom or Dad or Grandma or Grandpa have reached this new low in the Annals of Incontinence. And, yes, one of my adult children once asked my mother, *"Grandma, are you okay?"* I assured him that Grandma was fine.

TO KNOW: THE MIDDLE STAGE

For parents who aren't all that cognitively impaired, there's the middle stage of incontinence that I'll call *the gray area*. Assuming your parents can hold it in long enough to get to the bathroom and want to hold it in, their goal (and yours) is *to get there in time for the rump to hit the bump (the bump being the toilet seat).* That our parents succeed in getting to the bathroom on time or at least giving it that old college try is all that matters. And please, don't hold back if your parents need encouragement. Remind them about *The Little Engine That Could.* If you need to, recite to them, "I think I can get to the bathroom in time, I think I can, I know I can." And it is strongly urged (to pun it) that you adequately acknowledge success. Clap. Cheer. Be over the top. Give them gold stars. And enjoy this period while it lasts. Because it won't last. It's like bird migration. Here today, gone tomorrow.

TO KNOW

Your aging parent is like a preschooler, always needing that extra set of clothes *just in case* whenever he leaves the house. He also must be repeatedly reminded to go to the bathroom. But (to quote Shakespeare), here's the rub: how do adult children know when it's time for their parents to "go"? We don't. And we can't berate them for failing to tell us. Faulty plumbing and deficient memories are a bad cocktail.

IN SUM

As your parents' vital parts go, so goes their once-ironclad desire to control their basic functions. (*What is that expression? As Ohio goes, so goes the nation? Or is it Missouri? Whichever.*) Your parent needs to understand the number of steps it takes to successfully toilet himself. Even if he does buy into the concept, he won't remember to give himself ample time. And one day he won't even understand that toileting *is* a goal. So, remember: continence is a continuum. And it is definitely worth keeping your parent continent as long you both are able to. It's a team effort. Go, team, go!

Chapter 24

J: JEOPARDY!

No conversation about aging parents can be complete without mentioning our elderly parents' universal *Jeopardy!* obsession. Don't ask why they are obsessed. They just are! But I will bet you within two percentage points' margin of error (if a poll were to be taken), *Jeopardy!* would win as the favorite television show of older seniors, hands down, with *Wheel of Fortune* being a close second. Moreover, it's not just a favorite show; it's part of their lives.

To our parents, *Jeopardy! is de rigueur each day*, even well after they've lost the ability to answer even the most basic question. Maybe it has something to do with the blissed-out set, all plexiglass and bright that puts them in a state of blissed-out-ness. (Ditto for *Wheel of Fortune*.) Not to mention, Mom adored Alex Trebek. But, then again, who didn't?

AN EXAMPLE

Mom didn't just adore Alex Trebek because she thought he was a great host. She felt she knew him. She knew that he married late, was Canadian, had a late-in-life child and was an intelligent person who knew lots of the correct responses, even though he wasn't given the answers in advance.

Because Mom felt so connected to Alex Trebek and *Jeopardy!*, I saw an opening of sorts even though she was quite declined. While the show was on, we'd discuss the color of his tie and how his tie coordinated with his suit. We noticed when he had his hand in a cast. *(And it made him all the more relatable to Mom, what with her recent hip surgery.)* And I worried about him, and I continued to care about him, even before his diagnosis and even after Mom's death. I was grateful for him. Just seeing his face made Mom smile, and Mom was not what anyone would call an easy smiler.

Chapter 25

K: KNOW YOUR PARENT'S DOCTORS AND PROVIDERS

Whether your parent requires frequent doctor visits or not, you need to know your parent's healthcare providers. But bear in mind that their perceptions might differ from yours. If it is at all possible, try to meet those doctors, even if it's via Face Time, Zoom or some other meeting app. Then develop a protocol that works for communicating in a time-bound way. After getting a good sense of that provider, you may have to make a change if you feel something isn't right. Which may sound obvious, but isn't.

For instance, if your mom adores her doctor because he looks like Brad Pitt, but he's made some mistaken diagnoses or ordered some unnecessary tests or treatments, you'll need to step in. Or, if he shows a total lack of respect for your parent, you can't ignore it. If your parent is receiving good care from a doctor but your parent doesn't particularly love that doctor, that's a harder one, especially if that doctor has done right by Mom or Dad for years.

AN EXAMPLE OF WHEN NOT TO CHANGE DOCTORS

Mom didn't love her primary care physician. "His head is always in the computer," she'd tell me. This was partially true. But I also knew he was working on a new computer system and probably hadn't yet come up to speed. Mom didn't feel he had any other shortcomings. I liked him. He always communicated with Mom in a respectful manner. And his head wasn't in his computer that much during the visits, I observed.

There were several things that made me feel he was the right primary care doctor for Mom: He was knowledgeable. He was a good diagnostician, and he always explained his diagnoses and treatment in a sufficiently detailed way. He also returned my calls or emails promptly.

AN EXAMPLE OF WHEN CHANGING DOCTORS IS WARRANTED

By contrast, when Mom was in her eighties and fully cognitively intact, she had a primary care doctor who deserved to be dropped like a hot potato. I initiated the change. When I met him for the first (and last) time, he ignored Mom and spoke only to me. But the straw that broke the camel's back was the handwritten words I saw he'd scribbled on the outside of Mom's chart: "Pale. Obese. Old."

A nanosecond after we left his office, I urged her to find a new doctor. Reducing a patient to three insulting adjectives wasn't respectful. When he called asking why she changed doctors, we didn't feel we owed him an explanation. Was it our place to teach him about valuing his patients as individuals? Oddly, and quite beside the point, he was overweight. And I don't think Mom's weight at the time put her in the obese range. (*Okay, so maybe I'm getting a bit defensive about his description of my dear mother.*)

Afterwards, Mom told me she was glad she'd switched doctors. He'd made her uncomfortable on more than one occasion. A very private person, Mom did not appreciate being asked, "Are you dating?" It would have been one thing if he thought she was sexually active and wanted to remind her about sexually transmitted diseases. But she wasn't. He'd also wanted to perform a painful test which Mom refused and which, it turned out, was unnecessary.

TO KNOW: SOMETIMES YOU NEED TO RAISE A RUMPUS

Like some elderly parents who have heart issues, Mom was on a blood thinner that required her blood to be drawn at least once a week. Mom's regular phlebotomist, Justin, who came to the house at least once a week, was terrific. He always found Mom's vein the first time around, and he always came on time and when he was supposed to. But whenever Justin was out, they sent someone at the wrong time or on the wrong day who interfered with Mom's social activities and who was inept at drawing Mom's blood.

One replacement phlebotomist pricked her unsuccessfully so many times that her very caring aide ended the ordeal. I then called the office and demanded they send someone who knew what they were doing. It was only with the greatest of restraint that I didn't use a few choice four-letter words. But if I had, it would have been entirely understandable.

My theory is: replacement folks are almost never as good as the regular people in your parent's constellation. So be vigilant!

TO KNOW: HOSPITALS AREN'T SAFE FOR PARENTS (OR ANYONE!)

If your parent is hospitalized, you might consider staying overnight or paying someone to stay with them. Hospitals are not always adequately staffed, and not all staffers are competent. There are too many things that can go wrong, especially with older seniors who cannot adequately communicate their needs. Urine bags fill up, IV's run out and monitors malfunction. Also, if the dementia is advanced, your parent will attempt to get out of the bed if someone isn't at her bedside *at all times*. Moreover, with the advent of a new kind of doctor, a hospitalist, your parent's regular doctor will play little or no role in her care while she is there.

AN EXAMPLE

One weekend, when Mom was in a rehabilitation center, she developed a bad eye infection and there was no doctor on duty. Unbeknownst to anyone, Mom had put her cataract contact lenses in her eyes using dirty unsterile solution. (She'd had cataract surgery before the age of cataract implants. If she didn't put those lenses in, she had to wear unfashionable Coke-bottle-thick cataract glasses, which she didn't mind doing, *unless she had visitors* and she had visitors coming.) Mom's vanity trumped her now less-than-one-hundred-percent judgement. Within an hour or two, her eyelids grew red and alarmingly swollen. She looked like Rocky Balboa, at which point she was transported to a hospital.

Once she was processed in the Emergency Room, her regular ophthalmologist showed up. He told us the hospital decided to keep Mom there overnight and that he thought it was unnecessary, but he had no control. The only room the hospital had was a double room with a woman who clearly had serious mental problems. The woman ranted loudly all night. That night, I slept next to Mom on a recliner. It was not the first time I slept over in a hospital with Mom, nor would it be the last.

Chapter 26

L: IF YOU'RE A GOOD LISTENER, LISTEN UP!

Listening to declining parents can be a challenge. And it's not just because they repeat themselves. When they decline, their worlds become smaller and they're always good at holding up their end of a conversation. But I ask you: *do you really need to watch another adorable cat video?* But we need to listen to our parents. It makes them feel they are important. *And they are important.* It might be a good idea to read a book about conversation starters with your parents. Ours used to be about Alex Trebek's wardrobe. Yours can be about . . . whatever interests them, and there are things that interest them. Read on.

Chapter 27

M: THEIR MEMORIES BECOME YOUR MEMORIES

If your parents suffer from dementia and are still communicating verbally in a way you understand, their distant memories will come to the fore. What they choose to share varies greatly from parent to parent. But one thing's for certain: sharing those memories is a source of great pleasure *to them*.

AN EXAMPLE

Mom liked to recount to me the plots of books she'd read and movies she'd seen. Not only could she remember the beginnings, middles and ends. She'd tell me scene by scene, frame by frame in excruciatingly specific detail. She'd read and seen so many books and movies that *she could have easily been a top contributor to Wikipedia, IMDB or Rotten Tomatoes.* Sometimes, when I wasn't with her, I'd be reading a book and I'd have a weird sensation: I'd feel as if I'd already read the book. But I hadn't. Mom had told me the book's entire plot and it was coming back to me!

TO KNOW

If you can't see it through to pay full attention to your parents for long stretches of time, you must learn to fake it. Teach yourself an assortment of head nods that are so natural, your parents won't realize your eyes are starting to glaze over. At which point, you will have entered the *Automatic Pilot Zombie Adult Child Mode.* This is not a new skill. If you have children of your own, think back to when you used that same technique (or perhaps you still use it with your grandchildren) each time they insisted you read that same book, which, invariably, you detested. (I'm talking to you, stereotyping Richard Scarry, specifically *What Do People Do All Day! Ugggh.*) That technique should work unless your parent is on to you. In which case, be prepared to answer their pop quiz after they told you some movie's long and involved plot. *Mrs. Miniver. Now Voyager.* I know them all!

There was an upside to hearing a myriad of Mom-recounted story lines. As a playwright and sometime-fiction writer, I'm never at a loss for plots. So, thanks, Mom. It's the gift that keeps giving (*although my kids wish it didn't!*) I, too, recount the plots of movies and books to my children (the difference being that my very time-pressed adult children stop me at the pass). But, lucky for them, I don't have Mom's blow-by-blow elephant memory. (It skips a generation.) When I read a book, I can barely remember the last page I just read! And I wonder if the reason why two of my three children write and produce screenplays and digital content is because they were brought up listening to me and their Grandma retelling the plots of movies and books.

Chapter 28

N1: THE NAKED TRUTH— YOUR PARENT

Your aging, declining parents don't give a biblical fig about nudity, because they no longer understand the concept of the fig leaf, modesty or the famous Albrecht Dürer painting of Adam and Eve. So now you won't be surprised the first time you happen upon your parent stripping down to his birthday suit. It doesn't matter that before the decline, your parent previously had been one of most modest people on the planet and you never so much as saw a sliver of undergarment or other protrusions, except maybe a flash of breast or some other normally covered male or female part. Or if you did see something maybe once in your early childhood, it left an indelible impression, and not necessarily a good one. (Strict Freudians say even that one quick glance can produce lasting trauma. But I digress.)

But now that you are all grown up, you are too old to be shocked the first time you encounter your parent *au naturel*. So how should you react? Don't. Regard Dad's new clothing-optional preference as a No Biggie—no pun intended. *And resist the urge to buy him a getaway vacation at a senior citizen nudist colony.*

TO KNOW

Not to worry. Mom and Dad aren't contemplating a new career as a burlesque queen or bachelorette party hottie. And I don't recommend asking them (as I stupidly did) why they are disrobing in front of the big den picture window overlooking a busy residential street. If you do, you won't receive an answer. Your parent will merely smile and give you an existential shoulder shrug worthy of a sphinx or *Mad Magazine's* Alfred E. Neuman, whose slogan was "What, me worry?" They do it *just because* or because it feels good to return to the native baby state. It is why toddlers whip off their diapers. It is why the first time your aging parent does it, you are now prepared for it and you will respond with nary so much as a John Belushi raised eyebrow.

Or, if, like me, you've already bathed or showered your aging parents one or more times before they went nude-beach-style, the shock of seeing them unclothed will quite simply not be there. *You've seen it all already.* Just add this to the list of weird stuff they've begun doing!

Chapter 29

N2: SHOWERING THE NAKED PARENT

If you are showering your parent for the first time, prepare yourself: first, you gasp at the awkwardness of the activity. Then it sinks in, if it already hasn't, how helpless and declined your parent is. And then you realize that it *still* feels weird. It's that moment of truth when—*a drumroll is appropriate here*—if you ever felt you wanted to turn back you know there's no turning back.

You are a good child. And even if you decide to bring people in to help with your parents' daily living activities, know you have done something large and tender, and with the proper caring spirit. Feel good about having done it. And know, if you live to a ripe old age, even if you are a Pilates pro or a marathon runner, you still may bear a more-than-passing resemblance to how your parent looked in the *altogether*. And hope that your children will react not with revulsion but with a sense of purpose and filial duty when they bathe you. And don't give up your gym membership!

Chapter 30

O: RECREATIONAL AND SOCIAL OPTIONS EXIST. EXPLORE THEM

If you live in a municipality that has senior centers or other senior services, consider signing Mom or Dad up for some of their offerings, even if your parent never was a group person. Well-run programs are a resource, especially if they have programs for frail elderly adults.

And no offense: you may think you are a resource, but you're not *that kind* of resource. Don't wait until Dad begins doing funky things from a lack of stimulation. Unless he can't go outside because of health reasons or the weather is so inclement as to be perilous, there's no need to keep him inside all the time. Being stimulated and experiencing new things is of great benefit to a cognitively declining adult (and for all of us, for that matter). *Being inside one's mind all the time is not a good place for anyone to be.*

AN EXAMPLE

Since Mom had never been a joiner, I signed her up for two different programs. If we got very lucky—fingers crossed—maybe she'd like one of them. The first one was a general program for senior citizen of all ages. It didn't work out because there was a long corridor Mom had to walk down and she was only able to walk short distances. And at that stage, Mom would not have agreed to sit in a wheelchair even for a moment.

The other program, which Mom became a regular attendee at, was designed for frail elderly adults. It had a highly trained staff, a hot lunch program and a mid-morning snack (*and the latter two items might have been the deal-clincher*)! It also had arts and crafts, current affairs and classic movie discussions (which Mom loved but might have loved even more if she had worn her hearing aid)! There were holiday parties and the occasional outing.

The program also had an extensive intake process. It included an interview with the elderly person's family member and a home visit by a social worker who assessed the safety of Mom's environment. Thus, they had a sense of who she was from Day One. And I was relieved to hear that Mom's home passed the safety test. Whew! We had already installed a chair lift and grab bars in the bathroom, and many months before I had gotten rid of rugs and anything else that was a fall risk.

I admit, I was surprised at how much Mom bought into their program. My dignified Mom donned a long black fright wig they provided for Halloween. She happily painted ceramic figurines, although she'd never been artsy-craftsy. She even made extra ones for her extended family. A pink and white cat spoon holder sits in a place of honor beside my daughter's stove, and will continue to.

I don't know if Mom's willingness to engage in activities she previously eschewed was due to her cognitive decline or because having tried them for the first time, she discovered she liked doing them. Before her decline, she would have considered the ceramic figurines she made dust-collecting *tchotchkes*.

I admit, I was amazed at how my shy and retiring mother became an active and valued member of the group. And I cherish the letter the program director sent my family upon hearing of her death. It was a full-on appreciation of the person my mother still was. It touched upon her distinctive and special qualities, which all declining parents have.

Chapter 31

P: YOUR PARENTS' PERSONALITIES MAY CHANGE. BE PREPARED

While some declining parents' eccentricities increase with their decline, other parents' personalities morph into *something else entirely.* Fasten your seat belts. Mom and Dad can get downright wacky. But sometimes the way they change can be amusing, *although at first you may not see it that way.*

AN EXAMPLE

Before her decline, Mom had been a quiet, conflict-avoidant person. Her introverted nature (and fear of wrinkles) rarely allowed her to express what she was feeling, even to family members. *(Ah, the silent treatment! Memories!)* But that all changed when Mom declined. She began verbalizing both long-held and new opinions. One day, she described my outgoing, sociable long-deceased father as, "Voice-over, because he always spoke over me." *Suffice it to say, their marriage was not made in heaven!*

Often her zingers were directed at strangers. Perhaps she figured, hey, why not get a rise out of people. It's high time. Once, on a bus leaving a cruise ship I'd been guest-lecturing on, Mom politely asked a man who looked like Thurston Howell III from Gilligan's Island if he'd swap seats with her. He was sitting on the shady side and Mom was afraid of getting freckles. Mom's seat was closer to his wife, who'd been sitting on a different aisle nowhere near him. He refused. Mom perceived this as a lack of chivalry. She also was annoyed because the man's wife had just mistaken me for "the hired help" and had ordered me to carry her luggage! Mom told him, "Oh, I get it. You and your wife must have had a fight." I was mortified and flabbergasted.

In her earlier, non-declined state, Mom would have *never* asked someone to swap seats with her, much less offered an editorial comment if the person refused her request. But then I thought about it. Sure, hey, why not use some sarcasm, Mom? Go for it! Declining adults who have thrown all their inhibitions to the wind but whose verbal skills are mostly intact share what they are thinking. They no longer have filters. Mom didn't let loose that often, but when she did, she really let it fly and it always amazed and amused me.

Chapter 32

Q: QUIRKS CAN BE HARMLESS DELUSIONS OR PARANOIA

The more your aging parent declines, the more quirks he will develop. How many? Don't ask me to do the math, please. I got only as far as intermediate algebra. But trust me on this!

TO KNOW

Whatever paranoia your parents had before will seem penny-ante compared to what they develop. And although some specific quirks may relate to their pre-declined personalities, there are a bunch of common, almost universal delusions that folks with dementia have.

1. At some point, your parents will become suspicious even if they were the most trusting souls before
2. They will become suspicious of you
3. It may be a trusted caregiver other than you
4. If they live in an apartment, it might be the landlord or the apartment super
5. It might be someone they barely knew from forty years ago, who they haven't seen in the past twenty years

6. They blame you for things you didn't do, which isn't paranoia but it can still be very annoying

AN EXAMPLE

One day, well into Mom's cognitive decline, she told me that her rotator cuff injury was caused by yours truly. That was news to me, as she had never, ever accused me of causing that injury before her startling pronouncement. Mom had that shoulder injury for quite some time, and the only thing she'd ever told me was that her doctor felt she was too old to have it surgically repaired.

I tried to explain that I hadn't caused her injury. Mom wasn't hearing it, even though my voice was loud and strident. Mom had an alternate reality and I was the main character in it. (And if I really want to hyper-analyze why she blamed me, I did years ago close the car door on her finger, but we both knew it was an accident.) In short, there will come a time when your parents will wrongly and illogically accuse you of doing something. Don't knock yourself out trying to convince them otherwise. Just agree.

If they accuse you of taking away something you didn't take away (other than the car keys or some dangerous household object), just nod your head in a way that says neither yes or no and try to "redirect" them (to use the lingo of social workers). A great source of redirection is food, so feel free to offer them their favorite biscuit.

TO KNOW

Some fantasies/delusions can be funny to the point of being good material for a standup comedy routine. (I think of it in those terms, in part, because one of my sons is, among other things, a standup comedian.) Your parent may have always had some of those fantasies, only you didn't know it until now.

AN EXAMPLE

Mom believed that many people didn't like her, and she recounted to me every slight and injustice she'd endured. She'd say, "I don't know what I did to make the receptionist at the physical therapy office angry with me." Trying to convince her that the physical therapy receptionist wasn't mad at her was an exercise in futility. Finally, I came up with a new standard response: "Mom, if you just slapped a smile on your face, life would be oh-so-much easier!" Unfortunately for me, it took me forty years to learn that!

ANOTHER EXAMPLE

One day, while she was still driving, Mom returned from the grocery store and told me that S., the neighbor down the block who she'd played mahjong with for years, but who she hadn't seen for quite a while, saw her and pretended she didn't see her.

My analysis (which I believe comported with the facts) was:

a. Mom was mistaken. It wasn't S. who she'd seen. Mom had recently become blind in one eye, and although she continued to be incredibly observant to the point of still being able to spot a stray thread on her carpeting, she didn't see whoever she saw well enough. Thus, it was a stranger who gave her a blank look and not S. or

b. Yes, it was S., and their eyes locked, but S. was also in her early nineties and her vision probably wasn't that great either or

c. So maybe S. did see Mom and their eyes locked and she pretended she didn't see Mom. Granted, it wasn't nice but haven't we all done that at least once? Should Mom have gotten so exercised over it? No. Well, maybe. (After all, I am my mother's daughter's so I may have absorbed some of her glass-half-empty views.)

AN EXAMPLE OF MOM'S BELIEF THAT SHE WAS BEING DISSED

Once, when Mom was still driving, she came home in a state of high dudgeon. She claimed that while she was sitting in her car in the supermarket parking lot, she noticed Mrs. G. and Mrs. G's daughter in the car next to her. Mrs. G. looked at Mom, turned to her daughter and said, "Doesn't she look old?" Mom was convinced that:

1. the person who made the remark was Mrs. G. and
2. Mrs. G. was talking about her and
3. Mom accurately heard what had been said and
4. Mrs. G. wanted Mom to hear her rude comment

That it might not have been Mrs. G. who had made the statement, or if it was, she was talking about someone *other than Mom*, never entered Mom's mind. Mom was convinced Mrs. G. had dissed her. My analysis as to why Mom chose to attach Mrs. G. to a statement she possibly may have heard correctly from the adjacent car of some elderly woman she did not know is this: Forty years prior, Mom had been asked into a school carpool by Mrs. G. and some other mommies. But then, in the middle of the school year, a mommy who had previously been in the carpool prior to Mom's being invited in wanted back in. So, they dis-invited Mom (and my sister) from the carpool, thereby leaving Mom and my sister carpool-less. So, I get that "that was a lousy thing to do," to quote Mom. Agreed.

As to the likelihood that it was Mrs. G. in the adjacent car and she was speaking about Mom's appearance, I say *nah*. Moreover, I was convinced that not only did Mrs. G. leave the neighborhood years ago, she had gone to one of either two places:

a. Florida; or
b. "a better place" (i.e., she died)

I tried to remind Mom that there was almost no one left in Mom's neighborhood from her generation, (and I may have at this point been shouting out of exasperation). Nope. That didn't sway Mom from her false belief. I went a step further. I summoned Mom to my computer screen and together we googled Mrs. G.'s name. Sure enough, bingo! Mrs. G.'s name and address came up. She lived in Florida. We lived in New York.

So, that convinced Mom, right? No. Mom continued to hold fast to her version of the event, which only reinforced Mom's dual belief that

a. Mom looked old and decrepit, and that;
b. the world was not a kind place

TO KNOW: NOT EVERYTHING YOUR PARENTS TELL YOU IS FALSE

If your parent is in a nursing home, rehabilitation facility or some other group setting and he tells you a staff member did something inappropriate, do not dismiss what he says. Investigate. Ask questions of both the staff and your parent. Many, if not all, facilities have video cameras. In any event, it bears further investigation. If something did occur, that staff member may have asked other staff members not to report what happened or to be less than candid about what happened.

AN EXAMPLE OF A HARMLESS (AND FUNNY) DELUSION

Before I moved in with Mom, she told me someone rang her doorbell very early one morning, and when she peered out the window, the person ran away. Mom also told me that from time to time, her phone would ring very early in the morning. But when she picked it up, no one answered or breathed. From this, Mom deduced that it was the painter who'd painted her house several years before. Mom felt she hadn't tipped him adequately (which she still felt bad about) and now he felt it was payback time. I can only say that in all the years I lived with Mom, I never once heard the phone or the doorbell ring early in the morning.

Isn't it possible someone rang the doorbell early one morning? Sure. There'd been a few attempted robberies in her neighborhood. Could Mom's phone have rung repeatedly in the early morning? Yes. Sometimes fax machines call a wrong number again or it could have been a persistent robo caller. But was it the painter? I doubt it. But I didn't tell Mom that. I'd learned my lesson from my fruitless discussion with Mom about Mrs. G. (and which has now become part of my family's humorous lore). I empathized with her and told her not to feel bad that she hadn't tipped him enough. It happens! Pretending I bought into her version of events was oh-so-much easier!

Chapter 33

R: REPETITION, OR, DIDN'T SHE JUST SAY THAT?

So, your aging parent repeats herself, recounting long and involved memories of yore *(whatever yore is)*.

TO KNOW

Some parents' repetition is not a sign of dementia. Follow me on this: older people's recounting of signal events serves some kind of psychological function. But unless you are a trained psychologist, you're not going to understand what that function is. But no matter. When we listen, we gain insights into their minds and pasts. *But you won't hear me say these repeat-stories are fun to listen to.*

Just a reminder: in cultures where older people and dead people are venerated, it is considered the norm to listen to older people's repetitions. Some of those stories morph into important cultural myths or family lore, and the truth or falsity of the story becomes irrelevant. And in some cultures, there may not even be a word for dementia. *(All right, fine, so I made all that up.)* But I'm sure there's *some* culture out there that doesn't have a word or concept similar to ours for dementia.

The flip side is that, occasionally, some of our parents' stories are interesting. However, such stories are interesting only if they are re-peated no more than two times (two times being my personal limit).

TO KNOW

The stories your parents recount vary widely from elderly person to elderly person, except that they are almost always of ancient vintage.

AN EXAMPLE

Mom's favorite stories tended to be about her young adult dat-ing period when she was so beautiful that men fell at her feet. And I hope that because I patiently listened to her most of the time, my children will patiently listen to *my* stories. But I'm not betting the farm on it. My kindly time-pressured children cut me off at the pass, politely but firmly telling me they've heard that story. I tell them I am not losing it. I've forgotten which of my three children I already told the story to. And unlike my mother, my stories are never about my dating period, because I didn't have one to speak of. *The only men who fell at my feet were total strangers who tripped or happened to pass out near me.*

TO KNOW

If you're the family member who spends the most time with your elderly parent, by signing on to listen, you will find their stories are, *how shall we say,* not always of Oscar caliber unless:

a. Your parent was a spy
b. Your parent lived through a war or natural disaster, or
c. a and b or

d. Your parent hung out with oddballs, Damon Runyon Guys and Dolls types or people from the underbelly of life (whatever that is).

But know: your parent needs to tell That Story. If you tough it out and listen, you may be amply rewarded, although it may not be in this life. But, then again, almost all parents have a few dramatic stories.

AN EXAMPLE

Before choosing my father, Mom was engaged to two men at two different times *(or at least she said it was two different times)*. And before those engagements, she had a fair number of non-serious one-off dates, including a cowboy who was visiting New York and a religious student whose behavior was less-than, uh, religious. (He wanted to take her to a park nicknamed Kissing Park—Mom refused. *Or at least she told me she refused.* Just kidding).

Mom's favorite story was about Fiancé Number Two who, one night, got fed up with her continually putting off choosing a wedding date. He drove her to the edge of a cliff and threatened to drive off the cliff unless she'd set a date for the wedding. *(Oh, so now you're listening!)* She sweet-talked him into driving her home. Once she got home, she resolved to never speak to him again. He stalked her for a time, always sitting in his car, glaring at her whenever she left the house. I am happy to report my father was a far better choice.

ANOTHER EXAMPLE

Mom had another good story about returning from a summer bungalow alone early before her family came home and being chased by several young men. She escaped unharmed, but the men followed her right up to her ground floor apartment, and she could hear them right outside her window! Even if the stories aren't that good, you should feel special. Your parent chose you to tell that special story to. And if you are the only one to hear a heretofore completely unknown family secret, feel doubly special, and quote the Smothers Brothers: "Mom always liked me best." *Which may or may not be the case.*

TO KNOW

If your parents ask you the same question again and again within five minutes, even though you've answered the question, a visit to a neurologist is definitely in order. The doctor will likely perform what is called a mini-mental exam. The doctor will recite several common nouns, such as "baseball" and "cat," and then ask your parent to recall those words later. She may also ask some easy subtraction questions about shopping and making change. And don't panic if you forget one or more of those nouns. Blame your memory lapse on frayed nerves. *Besides, you can't decline. You are needed!*

I should add that I probably waited too long to take Mom for such an exam. I was shocked when she couldn't answer the doctor's easy math question, which was: if you had a dollar and spent thirteen cents, how much money would you have left? If I needed any additional proof that Mom had declined, I had proof: Mom fell asleep in the waiting room. In her pre-declined state, Mom would have never allowed herself to fall asleep in any public place. But I know I won't do that because I'm a drooler!

Chapter 34

S1: SAFE IN PLACE (WHICH IS A GOOD TITLE FOR A SONG)

If you've assumed responsibility for your parent, then it falls on you to make certain his household is elderly parent safe. Install grab bars in the bathroom; tighten all banisters and handrails and install a ramp and a chairlift if stairs are an issue. Make certain smoke and carbon dioxide detectors works. If you're not certain how to make your parent's house safe, consider hiring someone who knows how to. Your parent's municipality may have a free or low-cost service that evaluates your parent's home and may even make the needed changes for free or on a sliding scale if your parent is financially eligible. And remember: gravity and frail elderly bodies don't mix well. Gravity and any person's body of any age don't mix well!

AN EXAMPLE THAT OUR DECLINED PARENTS ARE AS HELPLESS AS KITTENS

One day, after I began living with Mom, I touched the kitchen light switch and discovered it was burning hot. I called the fire department. There was a smoldering electrical fire in the wall. Had I not called when I did, the house would have caught on fire. Mom used to have an amazing sense of smell, but even if she'd been able to smell it, she wasn't able to tell me she smelled anything. If she'd been alone (at this point, Mom was never left alone) she wouldn't have known what to do. She would not have called the fire department or 911. She no longer knew her address! She'd also lost the ability to use a phone, even if someone put the phone to her ear.

Of course, if you are a Nervous Nellie like me when I lived with Mom, you might find yourself calling the fire department when you thought you smelled something burning, only to discover that the funky odor came from a hanging exotic plant. I felt more than a little embarrassed when a full complement of suited up, axes-in-hand volunteer firemen showed up on our doorstep.

Chapter 35

S-2: SHOPPING MAY BE A PICNIC (FROM HELL)

If your aging parent is housebound, it will fall to you to buy their clothing. Which means that if they come from humble beginnings (and even if they don't!), they're not going to replace that faded and threadbare terrycloth robe they've worn for the past thirty years. So, do yourselves and them a favor. Buy some spiffy, practical clothes. By practical clothes I mean things that are easy to get in and out of (in case of whoopsies).

If you're still not sure you need to shop for your parent, peek into the closets. If the only thing you find that is remotely fashionable is a turquoise tuxedo cummerbund and a woman's blazer with shoulders as square as SpongeBob, a shopping trip is in order. Pick styles and colors that flatter them. Try to buy what they might have bought if they had seen it through to replenish their wardrobes. The grunge look doesn't cut it unless your parent is in a [senior] grunge band.

I'm a big believer that clothes matter. This may be because every member of my dad's family was in what used to be The Garment Center. The first question we all asked each other whenever we had a special occasion (except funerals) was: "What are you going to wear?" But even if I didn't have that background, I'd still be a proponent of making your parent look his best. Why?

1. It serves a positive psychological function for both of you.
2. Most frail elderly folks get smaller. Many of them shrink, and even if they don't shrink a lot, they lose weight, either from an illness, surgery or a fall. And they don't always gain the weight back, even with Ensure and other weight-boosting products.
3. Elderly skin is thinner than non-elderly skin so they get cold very easily. They need sweaters and sweatshirts or some extra layers of clothing unless they live near the Equator.
4. Our parents' (human) thermostats are faulty. They also may not be able to tell us when they are too hot or too cold. Which is why you need to buy layers.
5. If they still dress themselves without assistance, the fewer the buttons, the better. If you do buy clothing with buttons, choose large easy-to-button buttons. Think arthritic fingers, shaky hands and declining eyesight.
6. If your parents are still able to use the toilet (or even if they can't), pants with elasticized waistbands are a good choice. It makes dressing easier for them and/or their caregivers.
7. And don't forget about bras and underpants, if they are still wearing underpants. Who doesn't remember our parents' dictum to always wear undergarments in good condition because you never know when you could end up in an emergency room? The good news is, if your parent has moved from the underwear phase into the Depends phase, that's one less clothes item to buy!

TO KNOW

Your parent's life is ever-changing. Even one stint in a rehabilitation center or hospital will require loose-fitting clothing for physical therapy sessions. Also: hospital gowns are not warm and don't provide adequate coverage for the parts of the body that should be covered. Modesty counts, even if the concept means nothing to your parents now.

TO ALSO KNOW

Even if your parent wasn't previously a fashionista, unless she's completely housebound, people *will notice* what she wears and they will compliment her. If you've done your shopping well, feel good. You took the time, energy and expense to make your parent look her best.

AN EXAMPLE

Each time Mom was in a rehabilitation center, I bought her several fashionable sweaters. When I visited her, I took pleasure in hearing staffers complimenting her on that sweater with the little gold sequins and that other sweater with the fringes. Why have your frail elderly parent look less-than-wonderful when she can be a rock star? And it doesn't have to cost a fortune, either.

ANOTHER EXAMPLE

I visited a friend in her eighties who was in a rehabilitation center. She was one of those people who never left her house without her fake eyelashes and perfectly made-up face. She was beside herself because she didn't have any of her makeup items, so I went out and bought her some. She was overjoyed. She used every item I brought, including the fake eyelashes! The takeaway is: whatever boosts their spirits, do it! Smiles are a more-than-ample reward.

AN EXAMPLE OF WHY SHOPPING WITH YOUR PARENT CAN BE HELLISH

At age ninety-one, Mom needed a grandma-of-the-bride dress for my daughter's wedding. After she tried on many dresses in a large department store *(remember those places?)*, she finally chose an outfit for the rehearsal dinner. But Mom was resistant to picking a dress, *any dress at all,* for the main event, and the wedding was less than a week away. After what seemed to be forever, we agreed there was one dress she looked great in—and I wasn't faking my enthusiasm. With her dark brown hair and fair skin, she looked absolutely stunning in the champagne-colored tiered dress.

There was one glitch: Mom suddenly changed her mind and said she didn't want the dress. It made no sense, but then again, sometimes Mom's behavior made no sense. Parents get stubborn and irrational, even if they weren't particularly stubborn and prone to irrationality before their decline. Seeing my frustration, fellow customers told Mom how wonderful she looked. I was on the verge of tears. I ranted. I think I used a four-letter word. No, I know I did. Seeing me in such a state, Mom finally relented. Mission accomplished! After the wedding, she agreed the dress was a great choice. And I'm certain she didn't remember my *agita.*

TO KNOW

If a caregiver helps Mom or Dad dress each morning, you need to discuss (kindly but firmly) your expectation of how your parent should look whether he is in the house or out and about. And be smart. Get rid of ratty, frayed or hopelessly dated clothes. Otherwise, the caregiver may think it's okay to dress your parent in it.

Chapter 36

S-3: YOUR PARENT MAY DEVELOP STICKY FINGERS

Your parents' belief about what is and is not someone else's changes through time. Sometimes they develop an affinity for one type of item.

AN EXAMPLE: ITEMS OF CHOICE

To my knowledge, other than hotel towels [see below], Mom never took things that didn't belong to her. But now, in her declined state, all bets were off. Mom hankered after glossy art magazines that were always located at the exits of art galleries we frequented. Every time we were about to leave a gallery, I'd find a magazine in her hand, and she had no intention of paying for it. I put it back. Did she think it was free or did she feel that since she had one foot out the door, even though she walked slowly, she wouldn't get caught? I don't know.

Many years ago, one member of Mom's social group from the old neighborhood unabashedly bragged about how she'd attempted to pilfer a large hotel bedspread by stuffing it into her suitcase. It was only after being caught by hotel staff that the woman disgorged it. Come to think of it, that woman wasn't even a senior citizen when she recounted her story to the group. And I don't think that woman was cognitively declined either.

By comparison, in Mom's younger years, her pilfering had been low-rent. Whenever we travelled, Mom took towels from the hotels we'd stayed at. As a result, three quarters of our household's bath towels had the names of hotels embossed on them in large capital letters. One evening, after moving in with Mom, I devoted an entire evening to purging her overstuffed linen closet of what seemed to be an infinite number of white hotel towels and washcloths—they were always white in those days. Which is why, when I began traveling with Mom in her later years, I always checked her luggage immediately prior to leaving our hotel room or cruise ship cabin, *just in case*. Happily, I never found any towels. I guess the thrill of that hunt was gone.

To look at it philosophically: maybe Mom was just putting a new spin on the term "senior discount!"

Chapter 37

S-4: SUBTRACTION AND YOUR PARENT'S AGE

When your parents decline, they won't be able to tell you how old they are, but most of them can tell you how old they *think they are*. They'll say they are eighteen or thirty-five or some ridiculously young age. They'll say that their own long-dead parents are alive, which, even if they came from one of those remote yogurt-eating countries where people live to a hundred and twenty-eight, the math still doesn't compute!

Chapter 38

T1: TASTES CHANGE, USUALLY NOT FOR THE BETTER

As parents age, the things they like change. And sometimes it's a sea change.

AN EXAMPLE

As Mom declined, what she watched on television was largely determined by what her caregivers wanted to watch. What I found odd was, Mom seemed to enjoy their choices. She'd previously been an avid viewer of Meet the Press and daily news shows. But suddenly, she liked shows like The Young and the Restless and inane goofy commercials. While watching them, she'd call me over to watch them with her. Often, she fell asleep while watching them. Which leads me to wonder: if Nielsen can't distinguish between people who are actively viewing a show and those who aren't, shouldn't their motto be: "You (or your elderly parent) snooze, Nielsen Loses (the ability to accurately gauge viewers' preferences)." Just saying.

TO KNOW

Don't expect to understand why your parent's tastes change so radically, or what exactly it is that so tickles their funny bone. So, give up trying to figure it out.

AN EXAMPLE: THE PROGRESSIVE INSURANCE LADY

Mom loved the repeating character on the Progressive Insurance commercial—the woman with the black hair and red headband. Mom's favorite activity was analyzing (what Mom believed was) the producer's clever attempts at disguising the woman's expanding girth, which Mom attributed to the Progressive Insurance Lady's pregnancy. That set *me* to wondering why the producer had chosen to attire The Progressive Lady all in white, which is not a color that is good at disguising girth. That I spent time mulling over this, and occasionally still do, concerns me. As well it should!

AN EXAMPLE OF REALITY AND FANTASY MERGING:

Through time, your parents' ability to separate their lives from the lives of the people on television becomes increasingly blurry. Mom had a minor obsession with the man in the Trivago commercial. To hear her tell it, she had all the inside dirt on Trivago Guy. Mom told my son that when they first hired the Trivago Guy, he didn't look very clean-cut, but then they gave him a makeover and tidied him up. Had Mom wanted, she would have made an excellent creative non-fiction writer!

ANOTHER EXAMPLE OF MOM'S CREATIVE NON-FICTION

Not only did she like constructing histories of commercial actors; she loved creating narratives about real people she barely knew. Mom decided that the curly haired man and the curly haired woman who sat next to each other at the senior citizen center were brother and sister. They weren't. The woman in the hospital bed on wheels at the rehabilitation center was the mother of the center's owner, Mom said. (She wasn't.)

In the beginning when Mom told me these mini-tales, I believed her. After a while, I realized Mom spun these tales out of whole cloth. Sometimes, I foolishly tried to explain to Mom she was mistaken when I knew she was wrong. To use one of Mom's favorite expressions: *What difference does it make?* True. To this very day, I'm not certain Mom's narrative-creating had anything to do with her cognitive decline. It's possible she'd always created fanciful narratives. The difference was, she only began sharing them with me when she began declining.

Chapter 39

T-2: ELDERLY PARENTS REQUIRE TIME AND JEOPARDY!

Years ago, when hordes of mothers entered the workforce, there was a great debate regarding what was more important: quality time or quantity of time with children. Well, here's the thing: elderly parents require both in equal measure. Why? They like being with us, and we should feel flattered. For all I know, I may be the biggest dud socially, but when I was with Mom, she thought I was the cat's meow.

Regardless of how old we are, we remain at the very center of our parents' universe. If you feel that spending time with your aging parent is an ordeal, just remember: they saw you from Day One rump side up. They gave you enemas *(or at least some Baby Boomers' parents did. Or should we not go there?)*. They were in all the way and so should we be. Which is why, when we are with them, we should try not to engage in the non-stop multitasking activities we Boomers, Gen X, Y, Z'-ers and Millennials engage in. Multitasking has its place, but that place is not with our elderly parents. To use New Wave language: be present.

And lastly, and this is obvious, but I'll say it anyway: *no adult child of an aging parent knows how much time their parents have left*. Remember that.

Chapter 40

U: UN-REPLACEABLE ACTIVITIES (AND I DON'T MEAN YOU)

Among the many hats you now wear, add this large one: social secretary. So, if you don't already know how, you'll need to learn a new skill: orchestrating your parent's social life.

TO KNOW: EXECUTIVE FUNCTIONING CEASES TO FUNCTION

Whatever ability your parents may have had to make social plans and execute them departs. Former social butterflies are not capable of arranging anything more complex than the peas on their plate.

AN EXAMPLE

Mom never was much of a planner when it came to designing her days and social activities. She didn't attend meetings, classes or go to lectures. Nevertheless, she created routines that she found satisfying for most of her adult life. But as she declined, I felt she needed replacements for those routines. Even though she would never have signed up for senior programs, I knew it would benefit her, and it did. But it surprised me just *how much* she took to the programs. A smart, well-read lady, she always believed that the world wasn't a particularly friendly place and that if you hung your hat somewhere, if someone didn't steal your hat, they would silently mock you for your hat choice. Thus, I knew I'd have to do some extra work to increase the chance that Mom would successfully integrate into any group I would enroll her in.

AN EXAMPLE

When I signed Mom up for a frail elderly program, I made certain to meet with the program's director prior to Mom's first visit. I described Mom to her. I explained that Mom had read a lot and still knew and remembered a lot, but that she wouldn't put any of her knowledge out there without their urging and encouragement. I also told them that she would only return after her first visit if she was made to feel welcome and accepted right from the start. And so, bless their souls, the staff did whatever Mom needed to make her feel accepted from Day One and she went back. Success! I was so happy I wanted to do a silly dance (and I may have).

TO KNOW: OUR PARENTS' MINDS ARE LIKE AGING STRUCTURES

Declining elderly parents' minds are like well-made brick structures. With each brick that is removed, the structural integrity of that wall weakens. And it becomes necessary to find replacements for those gaps. In the absence of meaningful activities, declining parents will retreat further and faster into their deteriorating minds.

Chapter 41

W-1: WHEELS AND KNOWING WHEN TO TAKE THE CAR KEYS AWAY

Here's a simple rule: Take the car keys away from Mom or Dad before they hit anything that breathes, is a large or small inanimate object or is an unsolved cold-case file. But how? Everyone knows that getting the car keys out of a parents' hands is one of the hardest things an adult child can do.

TO KNOW:

If you attempt to discuss the subject of giving up driving, fasten your seat belts. Be prepared for lies, equivocations and evasions. Why? Our parents love, love, love their cars and will do whatever is in their power to avoid being denied the use of them. They understand fully that their independence is inextricably linked to their vehicles.

It's quite possible you won't take away their car keys the first time you have a discussion about driving. Chances are, that discussion will occur close in time to when you've suddenly noticed an assortment of dings and dents on their cars. Not realizing how compromised their hand and motor skills (pardon the pun) are, you may have accepted all the bogus explanations they gave for the declining condition of their cars. I know I did.

AN EXAMPLE

At first, I thought there was no pressing need for Mom to stop driving, even though she was ninety-one. Yes, her car had numerous dings on her back fender and the car hood was bashed in somewhat, but those dings and the hood bash had been there a while. Besides, Mom had explained each ding or dent to me in a way that sounded plausible. *(Okay, so fine. I am a bit gullible.)* And her explanation about the largest rear fender dent made sense: someone hit her car when it was parked in a parking lot and Mom was in the store and the person didn't leave a note. And besides, Mom correctly pointed out, it didn't pay to fix the dent because the cost was less than her car insurance's high deductible. Made sense, right? Um. Maybe not.

My mistake was not asking her questions about the bashed-in car hood. I assumed that the automatic garage door closed on her car hood because of a mechanical glitch while she was backing out of the garage. This analysis made sense because Mom was (I thought) still a good driver. When she drove me in her car, I'd marvel at her proficiency at gingerly maneuvering her large car out of its narrow space—there was little more than a few inches on each side separating her car from the garage door walls. More than once, I'd scraped the walls of the garage when I backed her car out.

Had I asked the right questions and not gotten acceptable answers, I would have been well within my (and the driving public's) rights to take away the car keys then and there.

AN EXAMPLE OF HOW LUCK MAY PLAY INTO GETTING THE CAR KEYS

One morning, while I was living at Mom's, I heard the automatic garage door open. I looked at my alarm clock. It was 6:00 a.m. I peered out the window. Mom was sitting behind the wheel of her car in the driveway. I dashed downstairs two steps at a time. Mom looked, well . . . not herself. She had an expression on her face I'd never seen before. She looked befuddled. (*I, on the other hand, being much more facially expressive, have an assortment of befuddled expressions in my repertoire that appear more often than I care to admit.*)

I didn't want to scare her, so I casually strolled over to the driver's side and tapped on the window. Mom rolled down the window. I asked her where she was going. She said she had a doctor's appointment. I asked her what date and time the appointment was and Mom said she didn't know. Unbeknownst to me, over the course of a few days Mom had become dehydrated. Oddly, or perhaps not so oddly, she didn't look dehydrated. Her lips did not look dry and parched. True, she looked somewhat pale, but she had ivory skin and always looked pale.

I asked Mom to slide over to the passenger seat. I hopped into her car, turned the engine off, and slid behind the wheel.

"Mom, let's go to a diner and have some breakfast," I said in a faux calm and cheerful voice. Her doctor's office was our next stop after breakfast. He told us she'd become dehydrated. And that caused her to become disoriented.

That very minute in Mom's driveway, I took the car keys away and never gave them back. And Mom never asked for them back. I know I really lucked out on that one. On some level, Mom understood that it wasn't just the dehydration that led to the car keys being taken away. It was high time for Mom to stop driving, plain and simple.

This began a whole new era for Mom and me (*and, arguably, the riding and pedestrian public*).

If you are not as lucky as I was, be prepared to have a Battle Royale when you take the car keys away. Your parent may rant or threaten to write you out of his will. Just tell yourself that it comes with the territory. And whatever you do, don't try telling your parent you are doing it for the greater good. If you do, expect a snort.

Chapter 42

W2: WHAT YOU MAY HAVE TO DO PHYSICALLY: BE PREPARED!

You may at some juncture be required to go *(Hmmm. How can I say this delicately?)* beyond the call of duty. Specifically, extreme constipation can be a life-threatening event, and health professionals might not be able to come often enough to address the problem and resolve it in a time-bound way. And time is definitely of the essence! And aides are not permitted to even consider the proposition that what goes into the human body has got to come out. In which case, it may be up to you to test the actual bounds of your love, devotion and manual skills to alleviate your parent's jammed-up-ness and avoid a hospital visit. I'll say no more except that having a large supply of surgical gloves in the house is an absolute must, as is wearing more than one layer for certain tasks.

Chapter 43

X, Y, and Z: ARE MISSING, BUT CONSIDER THIS MY CONCLUSION

I hope this book has provided insight into a journey that may be fraught but is well worth the investment of love, time, energy and care. At the end of the day, there's nothing quite so satisfying as knowing you did right by your parents. If you have cared for your parents well, when they have departed, you will be sad. But you won't have much in the way of regret. You may wish you had done some things differently, but there's also some consolation knowing you made hard choices for their benefit with all the available information.

When I stepped into Mom's life, her life became the center of my life. Caring for Mom was like being a mother of small children again, but not quite. As with child-rearing, I put Mom's needs before my own needs.

I became the hands-on chief decision-maker for all of Mom's day-to-day choices, even though, as time went on, one of my sisters acted as a sounding board and was a good advice-giver. She helped me make some of the most important choices, although we both knew that as the most-involved caregiver, I knew Mom's day-to-day needs and desires best, and she deferred to me on those matters.

The very end of Mom's life was how I had hoped it would be. Mom closed her eyes one weekend while sitting in a chair in her home while dozing in front of the television. Two days later, she died in her sleep. That I am not the same person I was before I undertook to care for Mom is clear to me. I am a more caring and empathetic person, even though I was caring and empathetic even before. Knowing I helped make Mom's last years some of her happiest years, despite her mental and physical decline, makes me feel really, really good. Not every day was easy—far from it! But I was there for her whenever she needed me. Mom's needs were always front and center. Everyone and everything else became a distant second.

I missed her terribly in the days, weeks and months following her death, and even now, several years later, I miss her still. But I know she'd be proud of me, that on the day of her funeral—which, coincidentally, was my birthday—I delivered her eulogy dry-eyed, clear-voiced and yes, stoic. A bit like her, I like to think.

AND FOR THOSE WHO LIKE TO
READ THE BACKSTORY THING

Divorced for a year, awaiting a buyer for my home while continuing to live under the same roof with my ex-husband without even one offer or doorbell ring—it was The Great Recession—I moved in temporarily with my mother. My motivation had little to do with her overall functioning or her age, which was eighty-nine. Mom shopped for herself. She went to her doctors and her once a week beauty salon appointment by herself. In short, she was an on-the-ball, independent older person. When I was asked by a reporter for AARP's magazine to describe our relationship, I said, "We care for each other." And, at the time, we did. I was already very much in her life, helping her with the normal aging-parent things: bill paying, visiting, taking her on excursions and trips, and arranging for, or doing, minor home repairs.

That I regarded my stay at her house as temporary was evidenced by my electing to sleep on her backache-producing non-pull-out den couch for the first six months I lived there. There was a large unoccupied master bedroom I could have slept in. Mom had vacated it before my father's death two decades before for reasons of, ahem, coldness (the room was the coldest in the house). There was another unoccupied bedroom I could have slept in, but I didn't even think to sleep there. *My stay was temporary, I thought.*

My immediate goal was to sell my house and buy a small apartment in Manhattan or Brooklyn, where I had recently taken a job and where my adult children lived. Mom and I had never really discussed where she might live in the future if she could no longer stay in her home. But I was determined to help keep her in her home if it was at all possible. Although she had never loved her neighborhood, she'd lived there for close to fifty years. Knowing my mother as I did, I knew she wouldn't thrive in any sort of group-living arrangement.

Before I moved in, I thought of Mom as being mentally and physically healthy, *despite her alleged chronic cold.* Not only was she able to remember what she ate for breakfast (i.e., her short-term memory seemed to be one hundred percent intact), she had a tremendous and accurate all-around memory. Sometimes she'd remind me of things I had zero recollection of, like the time we visited the Roman Coliseum thirty-five years before and our tour guide pinched our backsides through our winter coats.

And then things changed suddenly overnight. Entering her house following the successful launch of my humorous self-help book about parenting teens, *35 Things Your Teen Won't Tell You, So I Will,* Mom broke her pelvis. And while she was in the rehabilitation center recovering from her fall, I came to understand that large changes were in the offing. Mom was now mobility challenged. She was also, to a lesser degree, judgement impaired and she didn't fully understand the changes she needed to make in order to remain safe.

I had another large concern: once I began staying with Mom, she didn't want me to leave. We had developed routines, and even though I'd hardly describe myself as a barrel of monkeys at the end of a full workday and long commute, she liked having me there. And even though my quick weekday dinners consisted of just three dishes I cooked passably well in under thirty minutes, Mom looked forward to those meals, or seemed to. Moreover, even though Mom still drove, she began to go out less and less, and on some days, she did not go out at all. Often, within a short time after my arrival from work, Mom hinted that she wanted to go out to eat. *(Okay. So maybe the three meals I was capable of cooking weren't all that passable.)* After our restaurant meal, we'd head over to our local CVS, which had previously been part of Mom's ironclad daily routine. I jokingly referred to our after-work forays as Mom's "airing out," a description that Mom found hilarious.

And so, having no Plan B yet for Mom—I didn't even have a Plan A—I stayed on far longer than I ever imagined I would, even after my own home sold. My closest friends and my relatives encouraged me to remain in Mom's house. I knew I couldn't leave her in that big house alone. Did I forget to mention that the house was larger than your average suburban home? Which is to say, a large aging house has more things that can go wrong with it than a smaller house.

Another consideration was that Mom had no support system to speak of. She barely knew her neighbors, almost all of whom were a generation (and sometimes two generations) younger than her. And my two sisters were not there often enough to provide the needed safety net, and one of them lived two hours away. If I moved to New York

City, there was no one who would look in on her daily, no one who would notice if anything was amiss. That Mom didn't always answer the phone when I called made me worry about her safety. Moreover, she never mastered her cell phone, particularly the pick-up-when-it-rings-press-the-green-button-with-the-phone-icon-please-Mom part.

I moved in with Mom. My older sister firmly and wisely insisted I move from the couch into the unoccupied master bedroom. Mom and I soon fell into a routine. I taught her to play Scrabble, and even though she'd never played before, in no time at all she was beating the pants off me. Once or twice, she achieved the fifty-point bonus by using up all seven of her letters in one turn——Mom was a voracious reader and had a far larger vocabulary than me. Just one example: she knew what "hie" meant. *(Go ahead. Tell me you know it. Show-off!)* We watched *Jeopardy*. I soon began spending both days of the weekend with her, taking her on day trips to museums, historical homes, movies and concerts.

At first, Mom ambulated fairly well, looping her arm through my bent elbow for stability on the often-uneven sidewalks of New York City, where we sometimes went for our cultural outings. The weeks turned into months and the months turned into years. And even when a walker replaced my arm and elbow, and toward the end of her life, a wheelchair, I resolved that for as long as Mom wanted to go places and was well enough to go, we would.

Suffice it to say, I put my newly-single life on hold. If I'd wanted to meet a Brooklyn or Manhattan man, I was now low down on the Dating Desirability Index—*don't look it up. There's no such thing.* I now had a non-cool suburban zip code. But that didn't bother me one whit. Between my caregiving duties and job demands, I was bone-dry when it came to the emotional juice I needed to start dating. And I was more than willing to take care of Mom, whatever it took.

TO THE READER

Thank you so much for reading my book. I'm hoping you enjoyed it and had more than an occasional chuckle and belly laugh (and now, more than ever, we soooo need it.) I'm hoping this book raised your spirits and gives you hope that if I could do it, so could you. And you can!

What I'd appreciate greatly is if you could see it through to leave an honest review. Reviews are *way* more important than some readers realize!

Two such places/links to leave reviews are:
My Goodreads author link to Why is Grandma Naked:
https://www.goodreads.com/book/show/56656386-why-is-grandma-naked-caring-for-your-aging-parent

Or on Amazon, by typing my name, Ellen Pober Rittberg, or the title of this book, Why is Grandma Naked? Caring for Your Aging Parent or using one of my ISBN numbers:
ISBN 978-0-578-82862-6 (paperback) or
ISBN 978-0-578-84729-0 (ebook)

For those readers wishing to see what I am writing about and doing, and be in touch with me, my website is:
www.ellenrittberg.com
(formerly: www.ellenpoberrittberg.com)
Thanks.

One of the things I feel most proud of is that I helped provide my mother happiness and a sense of security both in the period before she declined, and throughout her decline, and I haven't pretended it was always easy. I am convinced that at the end of the day, it was well worth every bit of effort I put into it. Giving care and attention to our aging family members is one of the most important things we can do. On bad days, it's easy to feel alone and lost in the morass of day-to-day tasks. And the stresses experienced—*oh my*—they're different than many other daily stressors! In a nutshell, what I've learned is, what we give of ourselves reaps unanticipated rewards, and can be permanently life-changing (for the better).

For those who enjoy reading poetry, my full-length poetry collection, *He Is Walking Wider,* is scheduled for publication in June, 2021 by Kelsay Books. In it are two poems about Mom. Stay tuned, as they used to say.

Thanks again!

ACKNOWLEDGMENTS

To the three most wonderful children any parent could ever ask for: thank you for being there for me. Two of my children, Kim and Matt, read the manuscript early on and made great editorial tweaks, which were always on the mark. Matt Ritter is a screenwriter and stand-up comic who got the ball rolling by arranging for the book cover, and during a brainstorming session with me and his sister, came up with the book's title. Kim is an accomplished executive producer of TV and digital content, and little did she know I would be her most time-intensive pro bono client. Whip-smart and savvy, she lovingly and patiently served as my chief hand-holder for marketing and content strategy for this, my second published book but my first self-publishing effort. Son Jay has also leant his support in several important ways, and his great sense of humor and appreciation of the absurd helped tap into some incidents I'd forgotten about, such as the guaranteed laugh-line, "Is Grandma okay?"—see my chapter on incontinence.

To my sister Roberta, who was a solid sounding board and whose emotional support and practical solutions meant a great deal when I was at the end of my tether.

To my sister Stacy, whose late and kindly significant other, Rick, created a ramp leading out of the house, thereby affording Mom freedom to come and go as she pleased in the early stages of her decline, and for also maintaining consistent communication with Mom even though she didn't live locally.

To the staff at the Glen Cove Senior Citizen Center Frail Elderly Program for providing some of Mom's happiest social moments in the last year of her life.

To my dear friends Nora Yood and Cherie Goldsmith, who encouraged me to move in with my mother and cheered me on, and also to Rick Goldsmith, whose guidance and kindness were greatly appreciated when the going got rough.

To anyone who showed my mother a small or large kindness and to anyone who listened to her, gave her respect and smiled at her. She needed that. Don't we all?

To those professional companions and aides who tended to Mom with care, compassion and who took great pride in what they did. Thank you. G-d bless you. You know who you are. You made Mom's life better and I think about some of you still.

ABOUT THE AUTHOR

Ellen Pober Rittberg is an award-winning journalist and attorney whose humorous essays and features about family and social issues have appeared in Reader's Digest, HuffPost, The New York Times, Newsday, Boston Globe and other major media platforms. Her humorous self-help book, *35 Things Your Teens Won't Tell You So I Will* (Turner Publishing) was based on having three close-in-age teens  and not going bonkers. She represented many senior citizens and, in other matters, served as a guardianship court evaluator, making recommendations to judges. She has lectured on cruise ships, among other places, and has facilitated discussions about parenting and family issues in other venues.

Her full-length book of poetry, *He is Walking Wider*, will be published by Kelsay Books in June, 2021. Her plays, *Sci Fi* and *Sabbath Elevator* have appeared recently on New York City stages, in festivals and during the pandemic, on zoom. Her novel, *The Boy Who Could* is scheduled for publication in late 2021.

Her hobbies include walking at least an hour a day in order to be fit for other humans. She is also a birder/birdwatcher, spending a significant portion of that time getting annoyed at herself for missing the bird that everyone else saw. She wishes her grandchildren could be her hobby but understands that they have a habit of growing larger and require schooling, sports and peers.

Made in the USA
Monee, IL
24 September 2021

78709260R10075